# Sleeping With Wolves

Ken Fischman

Printed in the United States of America

Wolf N Bear Publishing
703 A Street, Sandpoint, ID 83864
ancientpathwaystoasustainablefuture.com

A version of the essay, "The Pleistocene Massacres" was
published in the Bulletin of Primitive Technology, No. 45, Spring
2013.

A version of the story "The Bear Hunter" was published in "The
Ides of Sandpoint" magazine, vol. 1 issue 2, 2005.

ISBN-10: 1534834680
ISBN-13: 978-1534834682

# BIOGRAPHY

Ken Fischman was born in Brooklyn, New York, and holds a doctorate in genetics. His last professional position was at Columbia University Medical School, where he did research on the effects of environmental agents on DNA and chromosomes. He has been a whitewater kayaker and founded the Columbia University Kayak Club. He was the first vice president of New York Rivers United. Fischman has taught wilderness survival skills and awareness. He has a longstanding interest in the culture of hunter-gatherers and the roles of predators, especially wolves, in ecosystems. His passion for Nature has led him to write and teach about a wide variety of environmental issues. He writes and publishes the website for Ancient Pathways to a Sustainable Future. He and his wife, Lanie Johnson, who is an artist, currently live in a cottage in the woods a few miles from Sandpoint, Idaho.

# DEDICATION

To Daniel Quinn and Tom Brown Jr., teachers who have inspired me and many others to go out and help save the Earth. My wife Lanie Johnson, who is my best friend and life companion, gave me support and encouragement for writing this book.

# CONTENTS

# INTRODUCTION

What do wolves, genetically modified foods, and the extinction of large North American mammals 10,000 years ago have in common?

This series of interlocking stories reveals a collective theme. Although each story is self-contained, in their totality they demonstrate a crucial connection between the natural world and the one that mankind is increasingly inventing, often without awareness as to the consequences for ourselves and the rest of the community of life.

I am a geneticist and evolutionary biologist whose interests include paleontology, anthropology, wolf biology, genetic engineering, mythology, and fly-fishing, just to mention just a few. By integrating insights into both science and the nature, these tales show that they are complementary ways of understanding and navigating the world we live in.

Ancient people were storytellers. Basically this is how they learned and taught, and here I continue this tradition.

Some of these tales are garnered from my own experience, and others I have gathered from quite disparate sources, such as American Indian legends, scientific publications, and East Indian oral history. In these tales I blend traditional lore with scientific facts.

Several themes in these stories, such as mankind's proclivity to deliberately and even inadvertently take over evolution, overlap to some extent; however, this repetition is intended to provide a foundation for developing a deeper understanding of these matters.

The first tale, "Sleeping with Wolves," demonstrates through my up-close-and-personal encounter with these enigmatic canids, the two sides of our relationship with nature: one of common origin and natural affinities, and the other of atavistic fears that cause us to attempt to control or destroy nature.

"Doctor Pusztai's Dilemma and the Mexican Maze" is a description of what happens when a few courageous scientists attempt to warn us of the dangers of genetically engineered food.

"The Tracks at Chauvet Cave" is a scientific detective story but one in which our growing concern for the safety of an unknown child, who lived more than 20,000 years ago, reveals that we are basically still the same people who gathered and hunted during the Pleistocene era.

I then turn to the related subjects of anthropology and evolution. The story "The Incredible Shrinking Megafauna" shows what profound effects both our deliberate and unintentional actions have on the animals with which we share the Earth. "The Pleistocene Massacres" is yet another detective story. Did we kill off the large North American mammals when our ancestors migrated from Siberia, and why is the answer of vital importance to us 10,000 years after the fact?

"People of the Earth" reveals the astonishing accuracy of a 7,000-year-old American Indian oral legend, and demonstrates that Earth-based peoples literally have some important things to say to us, if we are only willing to listen.

"The Fisherman and the Wolves" tells of my chance encounter with a seemingly jolly old man who suddenly becomes darkly angry. The tale shows how false and persistent stories, some of which had their origins in old European fairy tales, may lead to unreasoning hatred and a second extinction of the wolf so recently reintroduced into the Rocky Mountains.

The concluding essay, "My Son, the Indian," introduces us to a cast of charming and sometimes outrageous characters, who are leading a growing movement, dedicated to reconnecting people with the natural world.

# Chapter One

# Sleeping With Wolves

It was a dream job. In 2001, my wife, Lanie, and I had been chosen by Idaho Fish and Game to be summer caretakers and guides at their Stonebraker Wilderness Ranch. Stonebraker was situated 60 miles from the nearest road at Chamberlain Basin in the Frank Church River of No Return Wilderness, a 3.5 million-acre tract straddling the Salmon River in the middle of the state. We had many wonderful adventures there. It just shows how great a job you can get if you do not care how little you are paid.

The ranch was built in the 1890s by a German immigrant, Wilhelm Stonebraker, who horse-packed in all his gear. Many of his tools are now displayed on the outside wall of the dilapidated and swaybacked barn. If you look closely at the corners of the ranch house and outbuildings, you will see how the ends of the logs were painstakingly hand-cut with an adz and dovetailed together.

Spartan but livable quarters are found in one of the log cabins behind the main dining room/kitchen building and just down the hill from the shower and bathrooms. The furnishings are rudimentary and sparse, and the only heat in the surprisingly cold mornings came from the cabin's woodstove that I had to start in the darkness.

Nevertheless, we did have gas lights in the main house, a gas range and refrigerator in the kitchen/dining area, and running hot water along with flush toilets in the shower building courtesy of a solar panel that also ran the water pump from the creek in back of the hill. We even had a generator to run the washing machine. This was not exactly roughing it.

*Cabin at Stonebraker Ranch – Ken Fischman*

We chopped wood and carried water, as the Buddhist saying goes, continually repairing the old homestead and greeting its infrequent visitors. One of these was then-70-year-old Ray Arnold, the owner-pilot of Arnold Aviation, based in Cascade who brought in our mail and groceries every Wednesday by landing in and taking off from our cow pasture in his Cessna 206. We bribed Ray into telling us stories of his adventures, including his 13 crashes, by plying him with homemade chocolate chip cookies (his favorites) as he sat on our porch between flights. Ray is still flying his routes today. If you want to hear his stories, do not forget the cookies.

*Ray Arnold's Cessna at Stonebraker – Ken Fischman*

Our time at Chamberlain Basin was almost up now. September had arrived almost unexpectedly, and we knew that we would be leaving soon. The mornings already had the snap of autumn in the air, and it was crucial to fly out before the snows arrived around mid month. It was this realization that spurred my decision to camp out at least once.

The two of us had taken many hikes, but we had always returned to Stonebraker in the evening. I felt I had to do something about my lack of a complete outdoor experience in this special place before it was too late, so I announced to Lanie that I was going to camp out the following night.

I already knew exactly where I wanted to camp. I had identified it on one of our hikes. A wooded area about a mile away from the ranch and down two slopes was southeast of the pasture, where mounted visitors were expected to leave their horses to browse. There was a small, flat spot between two cottonwood trees which was directly above a steep 10-foot decline that led down to a little creek meandering out of the woods and through a wet meadow. It was an isolated and lovely place.

I carefully gathered minimum equipment and food, just a sleeping bag, some commercial freeze-dried food, a few pots, and some matches. No tent or stove for me. After all, I had been taught how to survive with even less by legendary wilderness survival teacher Tom Brown Jr. I was tough!

Lanie and I said our goodbyes at the ranch house door in the late afternoon, and I started on my way. I left myself about three hours to hike out, set up my camp, and cook dinner before twilight set in. It was a lovely evening as I walked, first through the emerald green and sweet smelling tall grass meadows, and then down the two drop-offs to the copse I had in mind. I was feeling so delighted that I was finally doing this that I practically floated down to the campsite.

I arrived in what seemed a surprisingly short time and proceeded to set up my rather rudimentary camp. I gathered an ample supply of dry wood from fallen Lodgepole Pine and dead branches jutting out from other nearby trees; I proceeded to carefully lay my tepee fire. A bird's nest would have made perfect tinder but not finding one handy, I used dry leaves and bark I crumpled and rubbed together. Next, I piled on matchstick-sized twigs in the form of a tepee, then several similar layers of continually larger sticks and finally a layer of finger-sized wood. This design not only made it easy to light, but would concentrate the hottest part of the flame at the apex of the pile, making it maximally efficient for cooking with the least amount of wood. I intended it to be a one-match fire, and I succeeded. I felt like a mountain man. I scrambled down to the creek to get some water with which to cook dinner. The stream, which was a tiny tributary of Chamberlain Creek at that point, flowed softly just below the steep bank.

Soon the food was cooking. It is a funny thing, but I had noticed on previous canoeing and camping trips that in situations like this, even ordinary camp food smelled and tasted as delicious as cuisine from an upscale French restaurant. It must have something to do with what they call the "presentation" in such places.

Well, Nature's presentation that night could not be beat. As twilight fell and the shadows from the trees lengthened, a soft breeze rustled the leaves high up in the cottonwood trees. I looked at the enchanting scene, down to the gurgling and gentle creek, across the meadow, and to the edge of a dark forest.

As I ate and savored the food, stars began to become visible, and the moon rose. What more could I want from a wilderness campout?

After dinner, I went back down the stream bank and washed my pots and utensils. By using sand that I scooped up from the creek, I was able to scrub the metal utensils until they gleamed like new. I was determined to do everything perfectly. I then walked along the top of the bank about 50 yards downstream from my camp and hung them up along with the next morning's food. Now they were dangling high above me on a tree branch where bears could not get to the food and far enough from my camp so any inquisitive bears would not disturb my sleep. Because I had even thought of that possibility, I felt quite self-satisfied.

Strolling back to camp, I felt confident that my precautions had also lessened the possibility of visits from other critters during the night. I snuggled into my sleeping bag, making a pillow from my jacket, which I had stuffed inside my wool sweater. The fire flickered and some coals popped a few feet away giving off a wonderful resinous pine aroma. I was very content.

As the last few embers burned with an ever-decreasing red glow, my eyes closed and I began to drift off into sleep.

Then, the wolves began to howl.

I was instantly wide-awake. I realized from the direction and volume of their howls that the wolves were just on the other side of the stream and meadow, probably inside the fringe of trees where the woods began. That meant that they were less than a hundred yards from me. A shiver slid down my vertebral column right to my coccyx, where my tail, if I had one, should have been. If, like most mammals, I had hair on my spine, it would have been standing straight up.

I was scared. Everything I really knew about wolves went right out of my head. Instead, images of Little Red Riding Hood played hide-and-seek with that of a ravenous wolf pack chasing a Russian sleigh while its occupants threw the baby to them in order to save themselves from being torn to bits.

As I lay there shaking, I realized that only a thin, summer goose down bag lay between my body and those crushing, razor-sharp teeth. I was trapped. Where was my .30-30 rifle, the one with the telescopic sight and silver bullets? Uh, oh, I did not own one! Well then, where could I go? Run for home? *Too far*, I thought. Climb a tree? Damn, these were cottonwoods and pines, with long slippery trunks, impossible for me to scramble up. Why was there not a friendly spruce nearby with its low, widespread branches? I lay there, struggling to keep my body quite still, but with my mind racing, trying to think of a life-saving strategy.

*Chamberlain Wolf – Provenance Unknown*

Well, Lanie will tell you that I can sleep through anything, and I proved it that night. The next thing I knew, the sun was warming my face and a gentle breeze stirred the cottonwood leaves above me. It was morning, and I was still alive! I woke with a start and looked around me. No wolves ominously circling. I breathed deeply a few times, unzipped the sleeping bag, got up and padded around the periphery of my camp, searching the ground. No wolf tracks. I collected my senses as well as the camping equipment.

I headed home, to Stonebraker. Ho hum, just another beautiful day in Idaho, but I had a good story to tell Lanie.

# Chapter Two

# The Tracks
# At Chauvet Cave

$T$ he two sets of tracks were side-by-side.

One of them was that of a young child and the other of a wolf.

These tracks were found deep within Chauvet Cave in the Rhone-Alps region of southwestern France. This cave contains some of the most glorious Stone Age art ever found. Some of the paintings on the walls of Chauvet date back to at least the Upper Paleolithic period, some 32,000 years ago. Among them are unforgettable scenes of mammoths, rhinoceroses, ungulates of all kinds, and even a leopard. One of the most striking scenes is that of a group of nervous, hard-breathing horses, with the adjacent wall showing a pride of maneless lions intently stalking them.

## *The Nervous Horses at Chauvet – archaeology.com*

My wife, Lanie, and I were viewing Werner Herzog's 2010 film, *The Cave of Forgotten Dreams*, which is a documentary about Chauvet. Herzog and his crew were the first nonscientists or technicians allowed in the environmentally fragile cave. As the film crew descended deep within the cavern, shooting as they went, we were enchanted by the beauty of the cave itself as well as the artistry of the painters. The cave with its paintings had been sealed like a time capsule, due to a rock fall some 28,000 years ago. It was rediscovered in 1996.

The entire cave is about 1,800 feet long and consists of several expansions, termed "rooms," some large, some small, connected by passages. Most of the rooms are filled with stalactites and stalagmites interspersed with curtain-like sheets of sparkling limestone. At one point the camera panned along the cave's dusty floor, showing bones of various animals strewn haphazardly across it. We also saw numerous cave bear skulls (*Ursus spelaeus*).

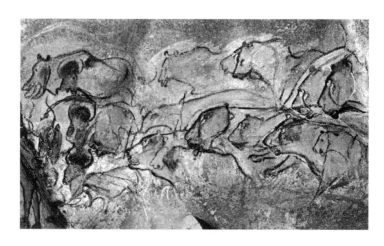

*Chauvet Lions Painting – unesco.org*

And then, within the stygian depths of the cave, the camera came upon the tracks of the child and the wolf. I forgot everything else at that point and focused on these like a laser.

Why were these tracks so intriguing? In the 1980s, Lanie and I took our first class in primitive skills with Tom Brown, the noted wilderness survival teacher. We went on to participate in several of his tracking and wilderness awareness classes, and we taught in his Tracker Family School. Tracking became one of our passions. We even tracked weasels under the snow in Manhattan's Central Park and pheasants in Inwood Park at the northern tip of Manhattan.

After we moved out West, I became interested in protection of endangered wildlife, especially the wolf. Living here in the Idaho Panhandle, a few miles from the Canadian border, I have learned a great deal about the biology and behavior of wolves, and we have studied and tracked them in Yellowstone National Park.

Herzog, whose iconic films include *Aguirre, the Wrath of God* and *Fitzcarraldo*, served both as director and narrator of the film. He panned his camera over the wolf and human tracks. Yes, I could see that they were side-by-side and was able to get an idea of their sizes and gaits (i.e., manner and pattern of walking and running), but the camera was too far away to see much detail. Herzog posed some provocative questions.

"Was the wolf stalking the boy?" he asked, "or were they walking side-by-side as companions"?

He also pointed out that the tracks could have been made simultaneously or a thousand or more years might have separated them in time.

Tracks can tell fascinating stories if you know how to read them, but these were enigmatic. Herzog's questions intrigued me and set me to thinking.

Unfortunately, the chances of anyone inspecting and measuring the tracks in the near future from up close are not good. Herzog was filming from a metal walkway, laid down some years before, about 10 feet from the tracks, and he was not allowed to step off the walkway and get closer to them. Too bad. It is possible to track at a distance, by the pattern of the gaits and registers. Gaits show the overall pattern of tracks, such as whether the front and rear legs alternate as do diagonal walkers such as members of the dog, cat and fox families, or are coordinated as in pace walkers like bears, beaver and skunk. I once witnessed Tom Brown spot and identify typically small fox tracks from across a pond simply by their pattern and register.

Register means whether the animal's hind foot steps directly into the front track, as do members of the cat family and foxes or makes its imprint a little behind and either inside or outside the front foot's print. You can actually tell the animal's sex in this way. A female mammal's rear straddle (the distance between the insides of the right and left foot) is wider than the straddle of her front feet because her pelvis is wider than that of a male of the same species. This difference is due to her wider subpubic angle, which delineates her birth canal.

You can, of course, tell much more about the animal or person who made the tracks if you are close to them.

However, the representatives of the French government, who control the cave, have "rules of engagement" that preclude anyone from seeing a lot of it at close quarters, for fear that they would disturb or destroy something vital. This is especially true of the cave's floor and its thick layer of dust, which they do not want disturbed.

This situation was frustrating to me as a tracker, used to examining tracks on my hands and knees, and seeing subtle aspects of them that give clues, even about the animal's state of mind and intentions. For example, close attention to details like the pressure release marks, which in a really clear track, show subtle changes that look like waves, dishes and disks, give an indication of which way the animal was shifting its weight, in preparation for changing its gait or direction.

None of these details were observable from such a distance, but still some information could be obtained from the quick look we were afforded. Besides, this lack of information does have the advantage of leaving me free to speculate about the tracks without fear of contradiction by uncomfortable facts that may be uncovered later. So, freed from those putative facts, I plunge into my own "cave of forgotten dreams."

First, you should understand that careful exploration of Chauvet had previously shown that although cave bears and other animals had obviously used it, no human ever lived in this cave. It was probably entered by humans only for the purpose of making the paintings and using them for rituals or initiations. The child's tracks, however, were found deep within the cave. What was a young child doing there?

The nether regions of the cave were normally pitch black. Until recently, there was no light in those parts of the cave except intermittently, coming from torches carried by humans long ago. Carbon traces from these torches have been found on the walls, and they have been carbon dated back to as far as 28,000 years ago.

Due to the necessity for light, it is almost certain that the perhaps 8-year-old boy or girl was not alone in the cave. The child must have been accompanied, at the very least, by one adult. Given the youngster's age, whoever accompanied him or her (we cannot determine sex from a child's tracks), was undoubtedly well known to the child and was most likely a relative. This reasoning is based on the fact that almost all contemporary hunter-gatherer groups consist mostly of extended families, and that these ancient people were probably similar in that respect. So, I think that we may all give a sigh of relief, confident that the wolf did not "get" the youngster.

Adding to this inductive reasoning is the fact that no child's bones have been found in the cave either. This should give us even more assurance about his or her welfare.

As for Herzog's question of whether the child and wolf were there at the same or different times, I am fairly confident about that situation, too. First, the cave is basically dry. It is situated high above the present course of the Ardeche River. Likely, the only water that could have reached it was through a spring, or springs, trickling along tree roots and through the rock. We also know that the tracks were made at least 28,000 years ago. That is guaranteed by the rock fall, which sealed the cave until its rediscovery. The preservation of the tracks for at least the intervening 28,000 years, attests to the fact that no water, mud or flood had ever reached them during that very long time.

An experienced tracker can "age" tracks and be able to tell whether they are a few hours, one or two days, or a week old, if she or he knows the characteristics of the substrate. Is it soil, sand, mud, snow? Tracks deteriorate at certain fixed rates, depending on soil type. The tracker also needs to be familiar with the environmental conditions too, such as whether it had been raining, or if the wind was blowing. All of that information was unavailable here. Besides, who knows what 20,000-year-old tracks look like?

It appears that the wet conditions, necessary for making these tracks, must have been a very rare occurrence in the history of the cave. For these reasons, I feel pretty sure that the wolf and the child had not been walking in the cave thousands of years apart. That would have been too great a coincidence. Most likely, they strolled together or had been there within a few days of each other.

I lean toward the companion theory for several reasons. For one thing, even the cursory sight we were afforded showed me that both the wolf and the child were just walking along with a normal gait. There was no sign that either of them was running, galloping or had even lengthened their strides. In other words, there was no indication of fear or panic in the pattern of the child's tracks.

Another aspect that I noticed was that the tracks never crossed each other or overlapped. If the tracks were made at different times, it is likely that they would have coincided, at least in part. After all, the cave is fairly narrow, and places where someone could walk are quite confined. There would not have been much room for their tracks to not come in contact except if they had been walking side-by-side, aware of each other.

Furthermore, from what I know of wolves, if this one had been stalking, it would have literally walked in the child's tracks. For example, when a wolf pack walks in the snow, they step in each other's tracks and do so with remarkable precision. This has the effect of breaking the trail, making it easier for the other wolves to follow the leader. Groups of human cross country skiers and snowshoers do this, too, for the same reason. It saves energy.

In this behavior, by the way, the wolf differs from human trackers who, on the contrary, are careful to not step on the tracks they are following. They do this as a courtesy to others who also may want to examine and follow this set of tracks. Wolves apparently are not as courteous but are more pragmatic than we are.

This wolf behavior reminds me of the flying wedges of geese, who essentially are "drafting" the leader as racing cars do. The following geese switch places with each other from time to time in an apparently systematic fashion so that they all take turns leading. This has the effect of distributing the hard task of leading fairly equally among the flock.

I do not know if members of a wolf pack tracking prey change places from time to time, but I have been assured by U.S. Fish and Wildlife Service biologists that wolves definitely track their prey, thus showing that they understand that tracks signify that particular types of animals have passed that way. For instance, they would not waste their time and energy tracking a grizzly bear.

By the way, I wonder if wolves can distinguish fresh or recent tracks from older ones. Such ability would certainly be of value to wolves because, once again, following old or "stale" tracks (especially if they were a thousand years old!) would be a waste of their energy. Conservation of energy is one of the prime characteristics of wild animals' behavior. Your pet Labrador retriever might fetch a stick out of the water for you dozens of times, but you can bet that you would not be able to get a wolf to do that.

A wolf can probably track both visually and olfactorily, having a much keener and more discriminating sense of smell than we have.

To return from this digression to the question at hand, it seems to me that the parallel tracks indicate that the child and the wolf were aware of each other's presence.

Whether they were companions is a more difficult question to answer. Present-day dogs are the descendants of wolves, but the information we have at present, mostly from DNA studies, indicates that the transition from wolf to dog took place in at least two different areas of the world at about the same time, some 12,000 years ago. One of these canine birthplaces was in China and the other in the Near East, both far from Chauvet Cave. So, both in space and time, it seems unlikely that this transition was taking place near Chauvet at the time the tracks were made there.

Nevertheless, we have to consider, for our purposes, that the transition from wolf to dog must have started, not with animal breeding, but with the taming of wolves. Most likely this was initiated by humans stealing or removing cubs from a wolf den. I know of no instance of an adult or even yearling wolf pup being tamed by humans. One of the most striking characteristics of wolves is their fierce wildness. Aesop's Fable "The Dog and the Wolf" indicates that this wolfy independence was a known and admired fact, way back in Roman times.

Wolf breeders know that if they obtain a pup early enough, it will regard them as its parents and will bond to them for life. Present-day hunter-gatherers and other Earth-based peoples are keen observers of their natural surroundings, especially the animals. The stories and myths that have come down to us from American Indians testify to that knowledge.

We can assume with confidence, therefore, that the Cro-Magnons of Chauvet were familiar with this aspect of wolf behavior and could have manipulated it to their favor, perhaps using such tamed wolves as guards or even aids in hunting, as present-day Botswana Bushmen do with wild dogs. Another important consideration in the companion or quarry question is that human beings are not the normal prey of wolves. There have been only one or two authenticated wolf attacks on humans on the North American continent in the last 200 years. Admittedly, of course, I cannot vouch that the situation was similar in Paleolithic Europe.

All of these bits and pieces of information and speculation have painted a picture for me of a child and a wolf, wandering together through Chauvet Cave while the adults were painting pictures or performing ceremonies. It is a nice image, and I aim to keep it unless new information arises to contradict it.

Chauvet Cave is a marvel indeed, opening to us not only a window onto the considerable artistic abilities of Paleolithic man, but also into his inner life, and perhaps in the case of the child and wolf, into his connections with the natural world.

I suspect that the story of the tracks in Chauvet Cave will always remain mysterious. After all, we are talking about events that happened a long time ago. Despite our careful analysis, it is still basically speculation. Perhaps that is what it should be. Sometimes a mystery is more fun than its solution.

*Two Rhinos Chauvet Painting – BBC*

# Chapter Three

# Doctor Pusztai's Dilemma

My phone was ringing incessantly. When I breathlessly reached it, I found my neighbor, Dr. Charles Benbrook, on the other end. "I have a house guest whom I think you might want to meet," he said. "It's Dr. Árpád Pusztai. We are having a get-together tonight at my house. Do you want to come?"

Did I want to come? Do cows give milk? Is the Pope Catholic? I had been reading about Pusztai for months in preparing for a lecture I was about to give on genetic engineering. The name Árpád Pusztai (pronounced poos-tee) is not exactly a household word, but in some rarified circles he has rock star status. He lives in Scotland. What on earth was he doing in the little town of Sandpoint, Idaho? I had better begin at the beginning.

Genetic engineering (GE) is the science of taking genes from one organism and inserting them in the cells of another, thus making novel combinations of genes that never would have appeared in the normal course of evolution. For example, when a gene for producing the pesticide Bt is removed from a bacterium and inserted into corn, every cell in the corn plant becomes a miniature pesticide factory.

Right from the beginning, there has been controversy about the nature of these new combinations, dubbed genetically modified organisms (GMOs), and their possible effects on the plants and animals in which they are placed and on humans who are exposed to them. Proponents of GE, which include agribusiness, many molecular biologists (scientists who do GE), and government agencies, argue that it will bring great benefits and is safe because GMOs are essentially the same as naturally occurring organisms. Its opponents disagree, both as to the so-called "normal" nature of GMOs, and as to their possible effects.

The question arises then: How can we determine if GMOs are safe to use as food and to let into our environment? One obvious way is to do scientifically controlled experiments on their safety. But because of the official government attitude that GMOs are a priori "substantially the same" as natural organisms, relatively little research into that question has been done.

In 1998, Árpád Pusztai, who worked in the Rowett Institute of Nutrition and Health in Edinburgh, Scotland, received the first grant in the United Kingdom to examine the effects of GMO food on animals. Pusztai, who fled his native Hungary during the anticommunist uprisings of the 1950s, is a biochemist who specializes in nutritional studies. He had written almost 300 scientific papers and has an international reputation. He was thrilled to get the grant. He did not know that it was going to destroy his scientific career.

Pusztai studied rats fed GMO potatoes, in which a gene from the Snowdrop plant was inserted. That gene produces a lectin, which is a protein that helps protect plants from insect pests by altering the structure of their cell walls. He thought that it was going to be a straightforward study that would support the conventional scientific wisdom that GMO plants were just like ordinary plants. He found instead that the presence of the gene resulted in stunted organ growth and produced immune system problems in the rats.

He sent off a paper to one of the most prestigious scientific publications in the world, an English journal, *The Lancet*. It was reviewed and accepted. That was his first mistake. The second one was when he was interviewed on BBC national television about his discovery. The head of the Rowett Institute called Dr Pusztai and congratulated him on his presentation.

Three days later, the roof fell in. He was locked out of his laboratory and subsequently fired. His wife and co-author also lost her job at the Institute, and the wrath of the scientific establishment came down on his head. Letters came pouring into *The Lancet*, criticizing his paper and also *The Lancet* for having accepted it. They ranged from charges that his controls were inadequate, his interpretation of his data incorrect, to insinuations that he had totally botched the experiment by mistakenly putting an entirely different, toxic chemical into the potatoes. The Editor of *The Lancet*, to his credit, vigorously defended the scientific value of Dr Pusztai's paper.

After weeks and months of such a bombardment, Dr Pusztai and his wife decided to take a vacation to get away from all the stress. That was mistake number three, and this is when the story really gets scary. While he was away, his home was broken into, and guess what was taken – his research data books! I wonder how much they would bring at a pawn store? At about the same time his former lab at the Rowett Institute was also broken into.

Perhaps the unkindest cut of all came when rumors

were spread that, yes, Dr. Pusztai had been an eminent scientist, but that now he is old and suffers from dementia. He had become addled.

Back to that evening at Dr. Benbrook's house on Upper Pack River Road. Chuck Benbrook ran an Internet information service, called Ag BioTech InfoNet. It was devoted to GE impacts and applications to agriculture, especially pesticides. Doctor Benbrook is an agricultural economist, who formerly worked in Washington D.C. as executive director of the Subcommittee of the House Committee on Agriculture. He met Dr. Pusztai at a conference in Paris, and invited him to the United States where he had arranged a speaking tour for him. (Benbrook himself is now under attack.)

I spent over three hours dining and talking with Dr. Pusztai. I found him to be charming, highly intelligent and surprisingly unbitter about what had happened to him. If he is demented, maybe we should all have Alzheimer's. He was as sharp as a tack.

### The Mexican Maze

University of California at Berkeley (UC Berkeley) graduate student David Quist went down to Oaxaca, Mexico, to show farmers how to test seeds for GMOs. Oaxaca is known as the birthplace of corn, and its ancestor plant, teosinte, still exists there. It was feared that genes from GM corn (or maize as it is properly known), might, by way of its airborne pollen, get into teosinte and the form of maize farmed there called criollo, and turn them into "superweeds," i.e. wild forms of domestic plants, that because they have been genetically transformed, with let's say built-in pesticide-producing capabilities, can successfully compete with their agricultural relatives and crowd them out. For this reason, and because transgenic (GE) crops are considered a particular threat to biodiversity, the Mexican government had declared Oaxaca a GMO-free zone.

Quist needed controls to show the farmers what both positive and negative results looked like. For the positives, he brought along store-bought corn from the United States, where at least 40 percent of the crop was GMO. He used native Mexican criollo for the negatives. But something was wrong. He kept getting positive signals from the criollo.

Quist took samples of the criollo back to Berkeley where he and his major professor, Dr. Ignacio Chapela of the Department of Environmental Science, decided to do more detailed studies. They came up with three major findings: (1) Much of the criollo had a Cauliflower Mosaic Virus (CMV) gene in it. CMV is a virus that infects and kills plants. It is used by molecular geneticists as a "promoter," typically used to "turn on" or activate inserted foreign genes; and (2) there was other foreign genetic material in these plants, and (3) most importantly, it had moved around in the criollo DNA. Genes are not supposed to do this. They are supposed to sit tight where they are put. If they move around, they could have different, unexpected effects.

Chapela and Quist submitted their findings to *Nature*, perhaps the most respected and tough-to-get-into journal in the world. Their paper underwent four rigorous peer-reviews in eight months, was accepted and published. The proponents of GMOs insist that GE is a safe, predictable and exact science. They give the impression that they know and can control where each inserted gene goes in the genome, and how it is expressed. They do not talk much about the possibility that these genes could have unanticipated effects or be passed on to other organisms.

This paper challenged all of those assumptions, and the reaction was not slow in coming. Several letters to the editor were sent to *Nature* by both present and former graduate students and others who had connections with the Department of Plant and Microbial Biology, across the campus at UC Berkeley.

Plant and Microbial Biology had recently signed a contract with bioengineering giant Syngenta, for which they received $25 million. In return, they agreed to do research for Syngenta and to put Syngenta employees on their board of directors. Even in these days of megabucks, this is a lot of money for one department. Quist and Chapela had been among a lot of people at the university who had opposed the deal, concerned that it would encourage research that favored genetic engineering and curtail studies that did not. We shall see how this plays out.

The letters were unusual for a scientific publication. There were the usual challenges about possible errors in: techniques, controls, statistics and interpretations. However, there were in addition, *ad hominem* arguments accusing Quist and Chapela of allowing their political convictions to sway their research conclusions. There were also allegations that they did not have appropriate scientific backgrounds to understand the intricacies of GE.

*Nature* ran an editorial that, for the first time in 133 years of publication, rescinded support for a paper; however, they did not ask for it to be withdrawn. In addition, in an unusual move, *Nature* asked Quist and Chapela to retest their samples using a different technique, and gave them a scant four weeks in which to do it. They actually accomplished this and confirmed their original results to the satisfaction of *Nature*'s reviewers.

AgBioWorld Foundation, a pro-biotech website ran by Tuskegee scientist C.S. Prakash, was a center for criticism of Quist and Chapela. It posted many e-mails critical of them, and curiously enough, 60 of the e-mails seemed to come from two persons, Mary Murphy and Andura Smetacek. This caught the eye of an enterprising columnist, Jonathan Matthews, from the British publication, *The Ecologist*, who succeeded in tracing the e-mails to the Bivings Group, a Washington public relations firm. One of Bivings' largest customers is another bioengineering giant, Monsanto. Bivings specializes in "Internet Advocacy" campaigns and "Viral Marketing." In other words, Bivings floods Internet postings and chat groups with anonymous or bogus correspondents in an attempt to influence opinions favorable to their clients.

Matthews discovered that neither Murphy nor Smetacek are real people. He also revealed that AgBioWorld was linked to Bivings on the Internet.

GMOs have become a multibillion-dollar business, very important to the AgBioTech industry and to the governments of the United Kingdom and the United States, which support these businesses. This industry has many allies in the molecular biology field, whose prestige, research money and very jobs depend on the public's perception that GE is a good thing. These institutions will go to great lengths to protect their investments, and they will oppose anyone who tends to cast doubt on the worth and safety of their discoveries. And they do not always play fair.

An analysis of these circumstances shows a clear, strategic pattern. Attack the dissenters' science and methodology through letters to the editor in scientific journals, websites, and press releases from scientific organizations controlled or influenced by the judicious use of industry money. In this way, divert the argument away from biological conclusions and toward experimental techniques. Make personal attacks, either upon the investigators' integrity or competence, or better yet, both. Finally, attempt to destroy their careers, thus preventing them from doing further research along these lines, and ultimately send a warning to other scientists that research into the safety of GMOs will not be helpful to their careers.

I will bring you up-to-date about Drs. Chapela and Pusztai. Quist and Chapela's results were confirmed by several other investigators. Soon after, Dr. Chapela came up for tenure at Berkeley. He was supported both by his own department and by the unanimous vote of the university tenure committee. In an unprecedented move, he was denied tenure by the chancellor. It looked as though he would have to leave the university. Protests were organized and letters circulated by students and faculty. Dr Chapela finally got tenure in 2005.As for Árpád Pusztai, veterans of the Hungarian uprising are not creampuffs.

They are survivors. Pusztai started an organization with a website devoted to telling about the other, darker side of GE.

# Chapter Four

# The Incredible
# Shrinking Megafauna

Wildlife biologist Doug Smith, who is in charge of the Wolf Project in Yellowstone National Park, said during a 2009 interview that he had recently seen something new and astounding. Several times he had watched a bull elk successfully fight off a pack of wolves. Smith said that the bulls had become so large and had such massive racks, that they were now a match for the wolves. What has happened in Yellowstone to bring this about?

*Elk With Majestic Racks - Unknown*

A fascinating, natural experiment has been taking place in Yellowstone National Park, ever since wolves were reintroduced there in 1996. By "natural experiment," I mean one that was unplanned and unforeseen. The last naturally occurring wolf in Yellowstone had been killed in 1927. Shortly thereafter, elk were introduced into the park. Lacking natural enemies, with the wolves gone and hunting prohibited in national parks, the elk proliferated over the years.

Elk population had burgeoned from 15,000 to 18,000 by 1996. They just overran the place. Then came the wolves, 45 of them. In the years since then, the wolf and elk numbers had changed drastically. First, the wolves increased, up to around 160 individuals, and thereafter had fluctuated periodically to between that and a little less than 100, while by 2012, the elk had decreased to about 5,000 to 7,000 animals.

You can say that the elk and wolves are participating in a dance of death. The wolves reduce the elk population by preying on them until the elk become scarce enough so that the wolves find it hard to maintain themselves, and that situation, together with other stresses, such as hard winters and diseases reduce the numbers of wolves. With less pressure from these predators, up come the numbers of elk for a few years until the wolves, with prey now easier to obtain, become healthier and less stressed and begin to increase again. This dynamic fluctuation has occurred several times during the relatively short span of years that wolves and elk have been interacting in Yellowstone.

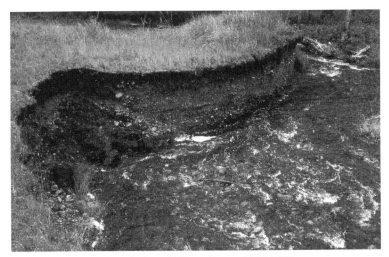

*Creek Bank Erosion - APTASF*

Other dramatic changes have taken place during this time. Dr. William Ripple from Oregon State University, who studies interactions between predators and their environment, has documented impressive changes in the Yellowstone ecosystem due to the wolves reducing the elk population. Elk used to hang out around valley streams, eating the succulent new tree shoots. The presence of wolves in the valleys has now pushed many elk into the relative safety of the hills. Riparian habitat (areas bordering bodies of water) has been restored, with willows and aspen again growing along the hitherto eroded stream banks, which have regained stability. Expanded tree coverage of the streams has lowered water temperature, bringing cold-water fish such as trout back, along with songbirds and many amphibians. The presence of more carrion, a byproduct of wolf predation, has proven beneficial to a whole string of scavengers, such as vultures, crows, ravens, foxes and coyotes.

*New Growth of Willows Along Yellowstone Creek -*
*Unknown*

But aside from all these changes, the one that strikes me from an evolutionary point of view, is the vision of these elk bulls with their majestic racks. Why has this happened?

From the point of view of genetics, the answer seems simple enough. Wolves prey mostly on the weak, disabled and sick, as well as on young bulls, calves and cows, simply because those elk are the easiest to kill. Thus, the wolves are removing genes for smaller, less robust bulls from the elk population.

If you think about it, hunters do the opposite. They go after the big bulls with the most imposing racks. Their success, therefore, removes the very genes they most prize and results in smaller, weaker elk.

In order to get an idea of this process, try envisioning the elk population as represented by a bucket filled to the rim with red and blue marbles. The red ones represent an array of genes whose activities would result in the growth of large, robust stags with huge racks. The blue marbles represent genes that result in puny bulls with small racks. Suppose that we start with equal numbers of red and blue marbles. This mixture of genes would result in mostly average size bulls. Wolf predation of elk would result in the removal mostly of genes for puniness, so remove half of the marbles but make sure that you take two blues for every red one. Now, refill the bucket with equal numbers of reds and blues, mix them well and again remove half, making sure that you take out two blues for each red again. If you continue this process a few times, the proportion of reds in the bucket will increase each time until the entire bucket has many more reds than blues. In this way, the proportion of genes for robustness increases in the elk population while those for puniness decrease, resulting in larger bulls with majestic racks.

Now, you may find it hard to believe that humans can have such drastic effects on wild animals. However, I have come across some other rather startling evidence that I think will convince you.

First of all, we can turn to the father of the theory of evolution himself, Charles Darwin. Most people are not aware that much of the evidence that Darwin accumulated for his theory was obtained through his observations of domestic animals. He was particularly interested in pigeons and became a pigeon fancier and breeder himself.

Along the way he became convinced that all pigeons in their incredible variety were descended from wild doves, an idea that contemporary geneticists, using DNA studies, have shown to be true.

*Charles Darwin, The Father of Evolution – John Collier*

Pigeons and other domestic animals were deliberately bred over many generations to attain characteristics that man wanted. This has resulted in the present-day cattle, sheep, chickens and even our friend, the dog, which was derived from wolves more than 12,000 years ago.

Among the main differences between domestic breeding and natural evolution is the speed at which man can produce a bewildering variety of animals and plants. Just look at the appearance and size of a Great Dane and the tiny Pekinese. Gene changes through evolution depend on the filtering effects of the environment to produce more of one variety of plant or animal than another. We speed up the process by deliberately discarding the ones we do not want and breeding only the ones with characteristics we desire.

However, what is even more impressive to me are the inadvertent effects that man has had on a wide variety of wild animals. The most startling one was the advent of the tuskless elephant. We know that most elephants have tusks, which they use to root around the ground for food and fighting each other during the males' rutting season.

A New Variety of Tuskless Elephant – Wikimedia
Commons

Historically, and from the study of fossils, we also know that about 2 percent of elephant bulls have been tuskless. This condition is probably caused by recessive mutations, which are gene changes that require two doses to have a visible effect. The loss of tusks put these animals at a disadvantage from their tusky relatives. Since these genes resulted in a disadvantage to the animals they affected, they were rare in wild populations. When a gene is rare, the occurrence of an animal with a double dose of it would be exceedingly rare.

The loss of these useful appendages has undoubtedly been the main factor, further winnowing out these genes from the population, and thus keeping the number of such elephants low – until recently. But what if the loss of tusks suddenly conferred an evolutionary advantage on elephants?

The number of tuskless elephants has recently climbed to 38 percent in Gambia and, even more startlingly, to 98 percent in one South African population. The factor that brought this change is the poaching of elephants for their tusks. The price on the market for tusked animals has risen to more than $10,000 per animal, and that is a lot of money, tempting impoverished African hunters and more recently revolutionaries who use the proceeds to buy weapons. In Asia, female elephants do not have tusks, but the proportion of tuskless male elephants has more than doubled in recent years, rising to greater than 90 percent, even in Sri Lanka, where male elephants are still used in the workforce, and their tusks make them more important for their owners as tools. Mario Festa-Bianchet of the

University of Sherbrook has been documenting this phenomenon and pointed out: "You end up with a bunch of losers to do the breeding."

Both sexes of these elephants are also getting smaller.

"These changes make no evolutionary sense," Festa-Bianchet said.

## A Whale of a Tale, or Floundering Around in the Mediterranean

Lest you think that these strange goings-on are confined to pachyderms, there is another, perhaps even weirder story about marine animals. It seems that fishermen as well as scientists have noticed that several different kinds of commercially valuable fish, found in the Mediterranean Sea, are getting smaller. Once again, the cause is obvious. Fishermen, using more and more trawlers, which employ dragnets that cannot distinguish between species or size, have made it a practice to keep only the larger individuals of fish such as groupers. After sorting the fish on deck, they often throw the smaller ones back, perhaps in the mistaken belief that they are being good stewards of the sea in doing so. They assume that the jettisoned fish will grow into larger ones and that they can catch them again in subsequent seasons. These fishermen could have used a good course in genetics.

This practice has resulted in the removal of genes for larger size from these fish populations, producing ever smaller and smaller cod, salmon, flounder and groupers, at least since the 1980s. Scientists have been curious as to how far back this trend of the shrinking fish goes. After all, fishermen have been plying the Mediterranean for thousands of years. Some researchers from Stanford and the University of Salento in Italy hit upon an ingenious and novel way to find out. They went to museums, examined mosaic tiles of Mediterranean fishing scenes from antiquity, and measured the fish depicted there by comparing them with objects in the mosaics whose size was known. Lo and behold, they found out that dusky groupers have been shrinking considerably for thousands of years. Even if the man-swallowing grouper in the mosaic pictured here is more than a slight exaggeration, it is obvious how far back the phenomenon of the shrinking fish goes.

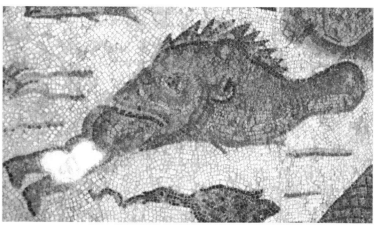

*Mosaic Tile of a Dusky Grouper – Archaeology Magazine*

Man's unknowing tinkering with nature is widespread. Bighorn sheep from Horn Mountain in Alberta, Canada, have had a 25 percent decrease in horn size because trophy hunters only go after the ones with imposing horns. In

Australia, red kangaroos have become smaller in size because poachers target the biggest ones for leather.

In the Caribbean, the size of fighting conchs (*Strombus pugilis*), a shellfish much prized for its meat (think conch chowder), has shrunk by two-thirds from late prehistoric levels. The change in size was estimated by measuring the shells in deeper layers of shell middens (piles of discarded conch shells left by native people) and comparing them with more recent ones. The good news is that in areas in which harvesting of conch is now prohibited, the sizes of these mollusks are already increasing, demonstrating that reversing thousands of years of inadvertent downsizing may be possible. Perhaps, it is not too late for us to learn a lesson.

# Chapter Five

# The Bear Hunter

Just north of Boise, Randy Wayne's red Maserati wound its way down from between the sear grass-covered hills that resemble monstrous brown dumplings. The road straightened out when it reached the city, and he sped down the arrow-straight avenue leading past the state capitol. It was a dark, early-December Sunday morning, so there was little traffic on the streets of the Idaho capital that could slow it down, and the driver, taking advantage of the situation, sped up, going through a just-turned-red traffic light and headed for the downtown section of the city. The driver began a conversation with himself.

*Confound that woman, I really will never understand why she always wants to hike into the forest. "I enjoy experiencing nature firsthand," she whines.*

Several times she had actually tried to entice him to go with her! No way. He did not want all that effort and discomfort. He found it disgusting the way she had to bundle up with boots, gloves, down coat, and that silly, red wool beret of hers.

*Now she's off again this morning. I bet that she'll be late to dinner – with Governor Crapo, for Christ's sake! Hmm, whenever we arrive though, she'll look great in that shoulderless gown she's going to half wear.*

He smirked.

*Jeez, that's why I married her. She looks so hot in those things, I get a boner just thinking of it. I saw his honor givin' her the eye last time we were at the mansion.*

By the time Randy arrived at the main entrance of a green, glass-enclosed, high-rise office building, wind-driven snow was beginning to swirl about its foundation walls and also around the cars parked at the adjacent curb. The winter's first layer of sparkling crystals was also parking itself on the sidewalk.

The middle-aged, overweight man, wearing a felt cowboy hat, striped scarf around his neck, and lamb's wool lined leather jacket, stumbled his way out of the car. As his embossed, high-heeled cowboy boots started to slip in the new snow, he grabbed the side mirror and regained his balance. He threw his keys to the doorman and scuttled manfully up the few steps to where the huge, automatic revolving door opened wide for him. He quickly walked past the row of elevators on his left and headed for another, narrower elevator door on the back wall. It was labeled in red "PRIVATE." It too opened for him, with a whoosh sound when the camera above it recognized his visage. Then it took him quickly up to the 18th floor.

The lavish but peopleless, dimly lit office had only one light on, a huge brass contraption hanging over a monster Scandinavian teak wood desk that rested on the far end of a plush, dark blue throw rug. Somewhere in the room a phone started to ring. It quickly cut off and he heard an English-accented woman's voice.

"This is Emily. It is now 0900 hours on the ninth of December, year 2026. Your Super Remote Teletronic Animal Harvesting Device has made a bear-kill at 0700 hours on this day in sector B345 of the Payette National Forest. Please refer to your electronic map for the best route to this location and contact me for further directions."

*Huh, I was going to go over those papers on the ski resort this morning that they better have on my desk right now! I'll make a mint on that bankruptcy, but it'll wait one more day. This will be good.*

He knew his priorities.

*This season I am going to get my head for damn sure! It cost me enough. I'll show those snooty Safari Club types what a griz looks like when I mount that trophy over my fireplace at the family ranch.*

He smiled when he thought about how he had outfoxed those guys and gotten the first grizzly hunting permit in Idaho since the Idaho and Wyoming senators had gotten the bears knocked off the Endangered Species list by slipping a rider onto a must-pass congressional spending bill.

*There's only 200 of them, and that'll make it even sweeter for me. That ticket cost me thirty thousand in the new Idaho Predator Hunting Lottery, but it'll be worth it to see their green-with-envy faces.*

He canceled his appointments for the rest of day and headed back up to his home at the very top of the "dumplings," the one with the huge American flag waving from the pole next to it. In the cavernous garage he exchanged the vintage sports car for a canary yellow $155,000 Hummer Special that was carrying a John Deere Spectral remote-control all-terrain vehicle in its bed. He hastily loaded it with a see-through sealed package containing, among other things, a canvas bag, orange plastic rope, a Bowie autographed hunter's knife with embossed ivory handle, and a small Husqvarna Diamond chain saw. As he drove the vehicle out, the garage door hissed open automatically and after a few turns, he headed north on Route 55, under increasingly lowering, dark clouds.

During the two-and-a-half-hour ride, he reminisced about the vicissitudes of the old days of bear hunting, when he had to use bait and dogs, and the failed campaign by those *"lunatic animal lovers"* to infringe on the constitutional rights of hunters to kill wolves and bears in the most efficient manner possible.

*It's too bad about the wolves though,* he thought. *They went too far with those open seasons, trapping, and helicopter hunts and they probably wiped them out.*

Despite Idaho Fish and Game's insistence that there were a few of them still up on the Lolo, he knew there had been no hunter reports of wolf sightings in the past two years.

*I never did get a chance to nail one, but a griz will make a better trophy any day.* He grinned. *It's bigger!*

He chuckled. *You can't stop progress.* He mused further on how cavemen used to hunt huge bears with only stone spears and pit traps, and how physically exhausting and dangerous it must have been for them.

*None of that for me. These new high-tech methods are a big improvement over '90s hunting. Now the odds are more on our side, and there is no need to get up at 5:30 a.m., bundle up, trudge into the mountains, and get cold, wet, dirty, like Becky is going to be today, and then likely not even get a bear,* he chuckled.

He thought with building excitement about how he

would use the new high-tech hunting devices he had just purchased, such as a remote sensing device, laser-aimed, computer-controlled, semi-automatic weapons. (The Feds had pushed through a ban on machine guns and rocket launchers after that Seattle stadium massacre during the COPA soccer matches. *Damn them.*) And a satellite tracking game locator that can be set for any kind of animal. Then he remembered with chagrin that the previous John Deere he had, sometimes misidentified the game animal. One time he took off a whole day to go up the Middle Fork of the Boise River, expecting to harvest an elk and instead found a beef cow!

"Holy cow!" he laughed out loud. But then he remembered that he didn't find it funny at the time.

*When I gave that dealer a piece of my mind, the guy gave me a real good deal on the new equipment along with a long-term warranty. That obsequious shithead assured me that the glitch in the harvesting software had been corrected in the new model.* "Why, we can even track woodcocks with it!" *It had better be. I paid a mint for it!*

Just then he arrived at the trailhead, and still in his cowboy get-up, he unloaded the Plexiglas covered, climate-controlled ATV and placed the package in it. Then he climbed in. He turned on the computer, touched a keypad and away he went, automatically being driven to his "kill."

Emily's silky voice cut in again.

"Now that you have put your ATV in kill mode and have become all comfy, sir, I need to remind you that there are a few things that you should be aware of. We cannot control the weather, and have found ... te da te da te da," she droned on amidst a burst of static. Finding the noise annoying, he switched Emily off.

*Convenient, I wish I could switch Becky off like that*, he chuckled to himself.

With the ATV unloaded at a trailhead, its computer ascertained the shortest way to the kill and maneuvered expertly through the heavily wooded area, despite the increasing snow, using its universally jointed, air-oil, independently suspended wheels to get over or around all obstacles, including fallen trees and mud holes. Randy sat back, mixed himself a drink and turned on the TV. Not finding anything interesting on the Terrorism or Game channels (formerly Animal Planet), he switched it off and his mind turned to how he and his wife had argued about this new hunting device.

*We seem to argue about a lot of things lately*, he grimaced.

"Excuse me, honey lamb, but it doesn't sound too sportsmanlike. Is it, honey?" He whined in imitation of her.

*Hey, I told her what for. It's the bottom line that counts. Them what has, gets. Nature don't have no mercy and neither do I.*

He smugly recalled that she had no retort but that he rubbed it in anyway. "Look at what my ways have gotten you. Hey, how d'ya like that new Givenchy gown I gotcha in Paris?"

That sure shut her up.

The ATV arrived at a shallow but steep ravine and abruptly stopped. It could neither negotiate it nor find a good route around the chasm due to the heavy alder thickets surrounding it and steep hillsides above it. Randy impatiently turned Emily on again and she informed him of this situation.

"I already know that," he snarled.

She went on sweetly to say that the kill was located only 30 feet away.

*Damn*, he thought, *I should have spent the extra money and gotten that model with tree-cutter capability.*

He cursed again because it had become more obviously windy and colder. He got out, unzipped the packet, pulled out and put on Mylar coveralls. He started to carry the canvas bag and chainsaw down into the ravine. His boots slipped on the snow-covered scree and he tumbled to the bottom, twisting his knee and striking his head sharply on a protruding rock, which knocked off his Stetson.

He regained consciousness minutes, or perhaps hours later, finding himself at the bottom of the ravine and in a full-scale blizzard. His head hurt something awful and he could not see more than a few feet ahead. As soon as he tried to get up he realized that his knee was hurt badly enough so that he could not walk, and he began to feel panicky. He tried to calm himself but soon began to shiver and drop into hypothermia.

He thought, *I've got to get back to the ATV. Order it to drive me to the trailhead. I can radio for assistance. Satellite tracker will guide the medevac 'copter to me.*

As he dragged himself laboriously up over the lip of the ravine, he lifted his head and saw a beautiful red fox standing in the snow, looking at him. He felt a strange kinship with it, but the fox just flicked its tail and calmly trotted into the storm.

"Wait, don't go," the bear hunter mumbled.

He looked ahead and dimly perceived an elongated, snow-covered form lying on the ground ahead of him.

*Damn*, he thought, *it's the bear. I climbed up the wrong side of the ravine!* "Shit!" he reached out to the form and grasped something that came away in his hand. He looked at it. It was a red beret.

He lapsed into unconsciousness again.

The storm grew in intensity. It would be very cold that coming night on the mountain, just as it has been during the winter for millennia.

# Chapter Six

# Pleistocene Massacres

History and pre-history are often best told in stories or narratives. There are two alternative stories to explain the extinction of North American megafauna (large animals) around 10,000 years ago. In one story, it was the advent of a land bridge from Siberia to North America, known as Beringia, created by the drop in sea level, caused by the burgeoning of the last Ice Age, that enabled Siberian hunters to enter and people the Americas. These selfsame hunters hunted the megafauna into extinction.

In the other story, climate changes, transitioning from the last Ice Age, set in motion complex ecological forces, which were responsible for the disappearance of mammoths, giant sloths, megabison, dire wolves, and other large mammals.

I believe that it matters greatly which of these stories you believe because they enter our cultural consciousness and are responsible, at least in part, in how we see the world. Our understanding of how the world has come to be, in turn, influences how we react to and treat the Earth. Therefore, it is my intention to examine both of these narratives, stating the evidence for each as fairly as I can, while recognizing that I, though a scientist, cannot be perfectly objective. I will then to come to some conclusions about them. In the interest of transparency, I want to state from the beginning that I have a bias toward the climate change theory, but I will endeavor to present both arguments as best I can. I cannot promise though, to present them with the same tone.

So, let us begin. In the first story, which I call "The Pleistocene Massacres" theory, there are two kinds of evidence, one chronological and the other material. It seemed to the first people who studied these extinctions, that the advent of the last Ice Age, the formation of a land bridge, called Beringia, between Siberia and North America, the movement of human beings into this continent, and the disappearance of megafauna all had taken place at roughly the same time. The apparent correspondence of these events forms the chief argument of the proponents of the massacre theory. This is impressive but circumstantial evidence. Is it sufficient to come to definitive conclusions about what happened?

Let us examine these events, piece by piece. First, there is the statement that the migration of Siberian hunters to North America and the extinction of large animals occurred simultaneously. Did they occur at the same time, and if so what does that mean? When events are concurrent, there are at least two possible explanations: In one, there is cause and effect at work. For instance, if a blizzard were to hit your town and a number of automobile accidents ensued, you might fairly assume that the icy conditions made it more difficult to control vehicles, thus bringing about more accidents.

However, sometimes when two events occur at the same time and even develop at the same rate, it is mere coincidence. There may be no causal connection between the two. For example, an article in a medical journal recently concluded that people who take large doses of vitamins have a greater mortality than those who do not. Did the vitamins cause these deaths or is it possible that people in poor health take more vitamins? How we distinguish between the two in our case is the challenge. In the so-called hard sciences, like physics and chemistry, the way to distinguish between two such possibilities, is to set up an experiment, using appropriate experimental and control conditions, and search for a plausible, and hopefully testable, statistically significant mechanism that connects the two conditions. Alas, in anthropology and paleontology, we usually have less evidence to go by and the opportunity to test these theories is much more limited.

My father was fond of telling me about the routine of a pair of old-time vaudeville comics. The first one would often tell an improbable story, a whopper, usually starring himself, and the other would challenge him. The first would reply "Vas you dere Charley?" Well, we were not there 10,000 years ago, and under most circumstances cannot reproduce the conditions in order to test their effects. I actually do know of one case, however, in which an ancient condition was tested. Coincidently, it involved one of the animals whose disappearance we are examining here, so I permit myself a slight divergence to tell you about it, both because of its relevance and because it illustrates the astounding potential of molecular biology to uncover seemingly long lost information.

*An Artistic Representation of a Woolly Mammoth –*
*Wikimedia Commons*

The animal in question was the woolly mammoth (*Elephas primigenius*). Some of these animals have been recovered intact from Siberian ice and carefully examined. One of the things noted about them was the intense network of capillary beds in their feet. Scientists reasoned that oxygen, carried in blood, was released in their feet to protect the animals from frostbite at temperatures that sometimes dropped as low as minus 60 degrees F. How could this occur when hemoglobin (Hb), the blood molecule that carries oxygen, releases it only grudgingly at low temperatures? The scientists speculated that mammoth Hb was different from Hb of contemporary mammals, but how could they prove this? First they tried the comparison method. They looked at Hb in the Indian elephant (*Elephas maximus indicus*), a modern relative of mammoths. No luck. These elephants have the same Hb that we have. Then they had an outlandish idea. Why not attempt to reconstruct mammoth Hb, using DNA, which they had obtained from frozen mammoth tissue? The DNA would contain the gene for building mammoth Hb. They grew the Hb gene in plasmids (circular pieces of bacterial DNA), gave it the appropriate precursors of Hb and wondrously produced mammoth Hb. They then proceeded to test the oxygen-carrying capacity of mammoth Hb at low temperatures. They discovered that the mammoth version of Hb gave up its oxygen at much lower temperatures than ours does and thus would have protected mammoths from frostbite. What shall we call this amazing feat of bringing back the distant past? Molecular paleontology? Or the Lazarus method?

In the absence of an analogous method by which to reconstruct the post-Pleistocene environment, and thus prove or disprove the massacre theory, we are left to sift the evidence, little and conflicting as it is, and to speculate, a lot. In addition to the chronological situation, the most convincing evidence for the massacre theory seems to be that there have been finds of enormous numbers of mammoth bones along Siberian rivers and on Arctic islands like Kotelny and Liakoff's, which lie off the north coast of Siberia. Massacre proponents believe that these bone troves are the work of human hunters. However, the Russian scientist, N.K. Vereshchagin found little or no signs of human activity associated with these bones. Grasping at straws – or more precisely picking up a few tusks that seem to have cuts in them – out of piles of millions of mammoth bones will not lead to scientific accuracy despite sensational media headlines engendered by massacre proponents. It would seem more likely that some cataclysmic natural event, such as a flood or storm can better account for these occurrences.

As I mentioned previously, the strongest evidence for the massacre theory is the assumption that when man first came to North America, the megafauna disappeared. In order to bolster their case, the proponents of this theory have looked at what they believe to be similar situations elsewhere in the world. They declare that the Aborigines accomplished the same kind of faunal exterminations in Australia shortly after these people arrived there, some 30,000 years ago. The problem with this line of thinking, though, is that it has been shown that the dates are way off. Most scientists now estimate that man arrived in Australia between 60,000 and 40,000 years ago. The question then becomes why did it take them from 10,000 to 30,000 years to kill off these Australian animals? According to anthropologists, and as stressed by Jared Diamond in his book, *Collapse*, the Polynesians wiped out many native animal species when they colonized the South Pacific islands between 400 C.E. and 1100 C.E. This account is undoubtedly true but it fails to take account of the special circumstances that make isolated island animals so prone to extinction.

One of the consequences of stressing this line of thinking is that ideologically oriented scholars and media have used it to argue that mankind is inherently predisposed to damaging its environment and exterminating many animals. First, let us examine the chronology of these events as scientists now understand it. With regard to the times that Paleolithic people first entered North America, about 12,000 to 18,000 years ago, and various large animals went extinct, these events may actually have occurred thousands of years apart. For example, the main massacre proponent, Dr. Paul Martin of the University of Arizona, stated in 1960 that the demise of the Giant Short-faced Bear (*Arctodus sp.*) in both North and South America took place around 20,000 BCE (Before the Common Era). However, among several other extinctions he cites, he also lists the American mastodon (6,000 to 8,000 BCE). He then says that horse (*Equus sp.*) bones were most commonly associated with man, but states that the horse became extinct in North America at 18,000 BCE. Therefore, there is a range of 14,000 years during which these extinctions may have occurred. Some of them happened 9,000 years prior to the 11,000 BCE Clovis Horizon, the advent of distinctive stone weapons that supposedly marks the entrance of Siberian hunters on the North American continent. The Mastodon extinction occurred at least 3,000 years before the presumed entrance of these hardy hunters.

There is yet another line of evidence, which I call evidence by analogy, that is derived from much later eyewitness accounts of American Indian behavior that appear to strengthen Martin's line of reasoning. There have been historic accounts from European explorers, traders and travelers, recounting that they witnessed Indians setting fire to prairies in order to change the ecosystems, and driving bison off cliffs for the purpose of collecting meat to tide them over the winter months. According to several massacre proponents, these acts establish that American Indians, who are the putative descendants of the

Siberian hunters, were destructive of the environment, bloodthirsty, wasted thousands of animals, and were clearly capable of wiping out North America's megafauna. These Indians, the story goes, are therefore no better people than we are today. As this story continues, the only reason that they did not totally destroy the fauna on this continent was that they had not perfected the sophisticated technology with which our society has quickly accomplished that sort of destruction, both in North America and elsewhere.

## *Evidence Against the Massacre Theory*

Loren Eiseley, was a respected anthropologist and chairman of the University of Pennsylvania Anthropology Department from 1947 to 1959. He is better known these days as the author of many popular science books, like *The Immense Journey* and *The Star Thrower*. Eiseley rebutted the massacre proponents, in part, by pointing out that not only megafauna died in these extinctions but that many smaller animals, such as birds, mollusks and frogs also perished. It is hard to conceive that fires, drives, spears and atlatls could have killed off such animals. Eiseley stressed, in particular, that 12 or 13 species of woodland songbirds perished during that time. Those extinctions certainly cannot be accounted for by the work of big game, Stone Age hunters, using only fire, drives, spears and atlatls (spear throwers). Eiseley also brought up the fact that many other grazing animals, such as regular bison, antelopes, deer, elk and moose, survived that period. Most tellingly, Eiseley stated that there is no evidence that any contemporary hunter-gatherers, or even tribal people, using traditional means, have significantly decreased or extinguished any species. As you will see, he was only partly right in this conclusion.

Predators and their prey almost always adjust to one another's numbers, with one increasing while the other decreases and vice versa. Classic examples of this dynamic equilibrium are that of Canada lynx and snowshoe hares in continental North America, and also wolves and moose on Isle Royale National Park, an isolated island on Lake Superior. I would add to this the population swings of wolves and elk in Yellowstone National Park, covered in more detail in my essay, "The Incredible Shrinking Megafauna," which have been intensively studied by Mark Hebblewhite of the University of Montana and Doug Smith, head of the Yellowstone Wolf Project. It is also hard to understand why the Paleolithic hunters and their megafaunal prey would not also be subject to what seems to be a natural law, that no predator can manage to kill off its prey because it depends on the prey for its own existence. Long before the prey would have become extinct, the predators' numbers would dwindle and eventually they would starve to death.

According to the Bering Straits land bridge story, the Siberian hunter-gatherers migrated over it to the New World. However, there is no evidence that these hunters eliminated many of these same beasts where they came from, in Siberia. And why did caribou survive there by the hundreds of thousands? The same is true for the European Stone Age hunters. Why would they have been able to do so in North America, using only the same or similar technology as their Old World cousins possessed?

It is also hard to imagine how such small bands of hunter-gatherers, presently estimated to have been less than 2,000 individuals arriving in North America, could have accomplished such a prodigious task. We know that only these small groups existed because molecular biologists have detected genetic bottlenecks (severe population decreases) by examining contemporary American Indians' DNA, and such people are the direct descendants of the Siberian hunters. It does not seem likely that such a small number of migrating hunters, using traditional weapons and skills, could have even made a dent in these extensive animal populations. It is also hard to understand why they would have attempted to tackle such formidable beasts as long as more vulnerable, smaller ungulates such as *Bison bison* and deer also abounded. Furthermore, so many other, non-game animals disappeared at the end of the Pleistocene that it is hard to argue that the Siberian migrants wiped them out, too. For example, extinction of many predators, such as the dire wolf and the *Miracinonyx*, a cheetah-like animal, which relied on speed to run down its prey, is hard to understand.

When European explorers arrived on the North American continent, they described a land that was teeming with game, and rivers literally overflowing with fish. One French explorer in the 17th century walked through what was later named Pennsylvania and described trees throughout his journey so huge that they shut out the sunlight and reduced the understory, making it easy to traverse the entire state on foot. What he was describing was basically a temperate rain forest. This is also true of the accounts of later travelers. Just reading the *Journals of Lewis & Clark*, describing the abundance of bison, bears and wolves on the Plains of North America, was an eye-opening and thrilling experience for me.

The Bartram brothers were naturalists who traveled throughout the southeast of what was to become the United States. I never forgot the image invoked by William Bartram's report of one particular episode. He crossed Florida's Saint Johns River in 1774 and described it as being so filled bank-to-bank with alligators that he could practically step on them. I guess that he decided not to attempt this feat; otherwise, I doubt that we would have his account. Two centuries later, there were so few alligators left that they were placed on the Endangered Species list. In the West, explorers and mountain men found the prairies, forests and mountains were in great shape. Were they exaggerating, as they often did in their stories? The amazing amounts of furs, which they often brought back, testifies to the truthfulness of at least these statements. How can this abundance of wildlife be accounted for? Did American Indians lose the skill and bloodthirstiness of their predecessors?

Large predators, such as saber-toothed tigers (*Smilodon sp.*), dire wolves, and spectacled bears (*Tremarctos ornatus*) also died during the Pleistocene extinctions. It is hard to imagine that Paleolithic peoples would have hunted down such fearsome beasts for sport, as some massacre advocates have speculated. Martin, in what was perhaps a fanciful tale, even went so far as to suggest that little Indian boys shot giant ground sloths, 8 to 9 feet tall, for fun. To say the least, this does not fit with the eyewitness descriptions I have read about the conduct of contemporary hunter-gatherers. For example, the children of South African Bushman are given toy bows and arrows (without arrowheads) and proceed to use them on rabbits and other small game with surprising accuracy. Needless to say, rabbits and squirrels make more likely game for 8-year-olds than do giant ground sloths. As I stated previously, it is not even certain that man's first appearance in North America and the disappearance of its megafauna were concurrent events. It is quite possible that these two episodes occurred as far apart as several thousand years. Scholars argue over the exact dates incessantly and it is clear after examining the literature that methods for dating long-ago events are neither standardized nor completely certain. Nevertheless, some dates can be established with more reliability than others, and the exact sequences of some of these events can be accepted as true with a degree of certainty. For example, the age of the first North American human migrations continues to be pushed further back into the past than the advent of the so-called "Clovis Horizon" hunters, indicted by massacre proponents, at 11,000 years ago. There are signs that a pre-Clovis culture, at the Aucilla River in North Florida existed around 14,000 years BCE, and recent excavations there show well-dated animal bones with butcher marks. Archaeologists are finding coprolites (fossil feces) and seeds at Paisley Five Mile Park Caves in Oregon, thus demonstrating the existence of a foraging economy there at 14,400 BPE. The Buttermilk Creek Complex in Texas contains pre-Clovis tools dated at 15,500 years ago.

The most important authenticated site was found at Monte Verde in Chile and is now authoritatively dated at about 14,400 to 16,000 years BCE. Since this site is 8,000 miles south of the Bering Strait, the ancestors of the people who set up what looks like a hunting camp there must have crossed over the Bering land bridge hundreds or perhaps even thousands of years earlier. There may be even older sites at Meadowcroft in Pennsylvania and Saltville Valley, Virginia, but their dates are still in dispute.

An astounding age of 22,000 years was announced by scientists in 2014 for a site in Brazil's Serra da Capivara National Park, near the part of that country that juts farthest into the Atlantic Ocean. There, amidst thousands of rock paintings, chipped stone implements have been found at a depth that has been reliably dated by thermo luminescence, a technique that measures the exposure of sediments to sunlight, to determine their age. If this date holds up, it finally puts a stake in the heart of the "Clovis First" theory, some of whose advocates have desperately mounted a rear guard action to challenge it by claiming that the tools could have been made by monkeys! They could not, of course, lay the blame on chimpanzees or bonobos, which are the only non-human primates that have actually been shown to be capable of making tools, for the simple reason that the nearest of these great apes are in Senegal, West Africa, an inconvenient 1,600 miles away across the Atlantic Ocean.

The significance of finding these earlier dates of human occupation is that it raises an important question of why these pre-Clovis hunters were unable to eradicate the megafauna, given their at least 2,500-year head start. On the other hand, it could be argued that their cruder lithics (blades, scrapers and choppers) indicated that their culture was not as technologically (and perhaps strategically) as advanced as that of the Clovis people, and that this made them less proficient at hunting.

There is another, perhaps more practical, reason to doubt the Pleistocene extinction hypothesis. To my knowledge, no one who claims that Siberian migrants killed off North American megafauna has ever attempted to kill a large and powerful wild animal, in the open, armed with nothing more than a stone-tipped wooden spear, stone clubs and stone knives. It is important to realize that these Pleistocene hunters did not have bows and arrows or even atlatls, and were not mounted on horses. On the contrary, according to the hypothesis, they were supposed to have also killed off these fleet stallions 11,000 to 13,000 years ago while hunting them on foot. As I previously pointed out, no contemporary observers were there while these events were supposedly taking place, so how do we know if this sort of hunting is even possible, and if so, how efficient it is? Here we are on firmer ground because some hard evidence of ancient hunting methods does exist, and we can also turn to present-day surviving hunter-gatherer and tribal cultures to see how they go about their hunting tasks.

*A Bushman Hunting With a Throwing Spear - APTASF*

There are many eyewitness accounts in the one continent where large herds of grazing ungulates still exist and smaller relatives of mastodons, woolly mammoths and rhinoceroses still roam free. I am speaking of the savannas and rain forests of Africa. European explorers of Africa in the 18th century, like Burton and Speke, gave many accounts of the hunting of these animals by African natives, armed with much better weapons than Pleistocene man had at his disposal. Africans were using metallurgy as early as 2,000 B.C.E., and had produced iron-tipped spears and knives by 500 B.C.E. They invented bows and arrows long before European observers arrived on the scene. They coordinated their hunts, using communicative and strategic techniques, some of which were borrowed from their observations of how jackals, hyenas and other predators hunted. Along this line of thought, we believe that North American Pleistocene hunters probably borrowed techniques from the wolf packs they must have observed. Certainly later on, American Indians admired and definitely copied wolf tactics. For instance, the Pawnee Nation's scouts were called the "wolf scouts" by other admiring tribes, due to their hunting proficiency.

By all accounts, hunting large animals on the African plains was dangerous, frustrating, time consuming and energy depleting. The majority of attempts met with failure. By the way, this is true for most predators, no matter who or where they are. We have accounts of !Kung (African Bushmen from Botswana) hunters tracking prey wounded by their poisoned arrows for over a day until they literally ran them down. Scientists who observe predators closely, whether wolves in Yellowstone or lions on the Serengeti, have noted that on the average, nine out of 10 attacks on prey meet with failure. I call this the "one-in-10 rule," since these numbers seem to be consistent for most predators the world over, with the exception of the dragonfly which has an astonishing 85 to 95 percent success rate. Nevertheless most predators have an enormous expenditure of energy and time for rather poor results. Stone Age man might have been more successful than animal predators, due to his strategic abilities and weapons, but he too undoubtedly met with more failures than successes in such difficult undertakings. Only a few animals were likely to be killed in such hunts, certainly not enough to even put a dent in large ungulate herds, which in the case of bison and caribou herds at least sometimes numbered in the thousands. Canada's Porcupine caribou herd can have as many as 180,000 animals when migrating. Such animals in Africa, even when poached with rifles these days, restricted in territory by the fences and other obstructions of agriculture, and challenged by periodic droughts, have obviously managed to survive in large numbers. A startling example is the wildebeest migration of 1.5 million animals.

This brings us to the subject of buffalo jumps. These jumps were usually cliffs over which American Indians would attempt to stampede bison herds, in order to drive them to their deaths, thus being able to make use of their meat and hides. Some massacre proponents have cited these jumps as examples of "primitive" people's ability to employ systematic and efficient methods of killing large numbers of prey animals. Apparently, there were a good many such places in the American West, and we know of some of their locations.

I traveled to the Madison River in western Montana, in order to examine one of these places, now called Madison Buffalo Jump State Park. It was impressive, quite beautiful with sheer 30-foot cliffs on three sides, and had apparently been used by American Indian hunters for thousands of years. Areas directly adjacent to these cliffs had been used for skinning the bison, dressing the meat and smoking it, probably in order to preserve it through the long, cold and snowy winters prevalent in that part of the Rockies.

*Buffalo Jump in Montana – Ken Fischman*

Using these tactics, hunters were able to kill large numbers of bison with less effort than hunting them from horseback with bows and arrows, a method that wasn't available to Paleolithic hunters. Some scholars also point out the waste of such a method, which often left many more dead animals than the hunters could butcher and use. Those critics make two anti-Pleistocene hunter criticisms at once: one, that these hunters were indeed capable of killing large numbers of animals; and two, that they wasted resources. The trouble with these accusations is that they do not appear to stand up to scrutiny. The critics state that these methods were widespread. If so, how successful were the Indians in wiping out the bison? As I pointed out, the Indians had employed these methods for thousands of years, without even making a dent in the bison population. The existence of such places is evidence that even the use of such sophisticated hunting techniques failed to wipe out these animals. By all accounts, enormous herds of bison, from a population which some have estimated at 50 million to 60 million animals, still roamed the American West, even in the 1800s.

In addition, why should we assume that the Siberian Neolithic migrants to North America, who were the predecessors of American Indians but had a much smaller population, had been more successful in exterminating the much larger and presumably more dangerous bison (*Bison antiquus*) when their ancestors had been unable to do so in Siberia? And how did these Neolithic hunters accomplish the permanent demise of dozens of species of other megafauna? No evidence exists that other animals, such as woolly mammoths and giant sloths, were susceptible to stampede methods. How did the paleohunters, for instance, wipe out the large ungulates such as *Bison antiquus* when horse-mounted Indians were unable to do so with their smaller descendents, *Bison bison*? Were their Pleistocene predecessors more clever than they? Hardly likely. As for the criticism about wasting the meat from animals killed at buffalo jumps, none of the critics have explained how Indians could have limited the numbers of animals killed using this crude but effective strategy. Needless to say, our Euro-American ancestors who shot bison for sport from moving trains could have easily limited the numbers killed by that method, but they did not. In fact, they left the corpses of thousands of bison to rot on the Western plains as their trains moved on.

Also, the Indians exerted enormous amounts of energy in skinning bison, stripping and drying their meat in order to store it, and tanning their hides for use as clothing, tepees and preparing bone tools, such as awls, and sinews for sewing the skins together. Anyone who has ever tried hand tanning, even with a much smaller and thinner-skinned animal such as a deer, as yours truly has, can testify that this is a backbreaking and time-consuming task.

*Pile of Bison Skulls – Rare Historical Photos*

In addition to these senseless killings, it is well known that the wanton killing of American bison was a deliberate and overt tactic employed by our government to remove an animal absolutely essential to the lifestyle and spiritual well-being of Plains Indians. The loss of the bison forced American Indians onto reservations and opened up the plains states to private property, ranching and agriculture. No such motivation can be attributed to the paleohunters, who were just looking for meat and sustenance.

Observations of native African hunters afford us another opportunity to evaluate the hunting methods of indigenous people, this one of comparison. How did these hunters fare? Prior to the advent of Bantu agriculturalists and white European colonists in the 19th and 20th centuries, the Bushmen inhabited the entire region of South Africa. Recent genetic and archaeological evidence shows that the Bushmen are descended from the oldest line of human evolution. Therefore, they have been hunting in this region for tens of thousands of years. According to their own rock paintings and other archaeological evidence, Bushmen hunted large ungulates on foot and employed bows with poison-tipped arrows as early as 24,000 years ago. That would seem like a neat, efficient way to dispatch large ungulates, but as they say, the devil is in the details. Bushmen first had to stalk near enough to edgy herds in order to use their weapons with any kind of accuracy. The small amount of poison dabbed on arrowheads worked slowly in such large animals. The hunters, therefore, had to follow or track the wounded animal for hours and sometimes even days before the animal died. The documentary film *The Great Dance* shows Bushman actually running after these animals all day until they exhausted and cornered them. The stamina of Iron Man competitors and ultra marathoners pales in comparison to that of these hunters. They were then faced with the task of butchering the animal on the spot, and thus heavily laden, had to carry the meat back to their extended families at their temporary encampments. Keep in mind that the Bushmen are little fellows, most of them barely over 5 feet tall. Any elk hunter, who has ever shot an elk on top of the mountain or far off the road, can testify as to what a challenging task this is.

The Babenzele pygmies of Zaire's northeastern rain forests, have perfected a skillful way to hunt in heavily forested areas. It is a cooperative hunt using nets made from nicusa vine (*Manniophyton*) cordage. The entire group, made up of an extended family, participates. Each nuclear family subunit of the group is responsible for one section of net, about as high as a volleyball net but much longer, that they must keep in good repair. They put the nets together end to end and bend the entire apparatus into the form of a horseshoe-shaped trap covering several acres by tying it to trees and bushes.

Other members of their families, including women and children, then drive the animals into the open end of the trap by shouting, pounding trees with sticks and altogether making as much noise as possible. In this manner they can trap and kill small animals, such as pygmy deer and duikers, in an efficient manner. You could consider this method as a rainforest equivalent of a buffalo jump, but it is certainly no way to wipe out the entire forest fauna and obviously, hunting in this way for millennia, they have not done so.

Pygmies are genetically related to Bushmen, and like them, are descendants of the most ancient human lineage in the world. Anthropologists had long suspected pygmy ethnic antiquity from examining their culture. Recently, DNA studies have confirmed the lineage and racial interrelationships of the various pygmy groups, such as the Baka and Mbuti, even though these peoples are separated from each other by more than a thousand miles of forest.

This is evidence of the cohesiveness and relative exclusivity of their cultures and ancestry. Pygmies are also reputed to be efficient and courageous hunters of forest elephants (*Loxodonta cyclotis*), which they hunt with spears. These animals are a smaller version of those in large herds (*Loxodonta africana*) that roam the African Savannah.

*Pygmy With Hunting Net – Nigil Pavitt*

Massacre proponents recite virtually the same scenario for the continent of Australia as they do for North America and use this information as further validation of the bloodthirsty efficiency of primitive hunters. That is, when humans arrived in Australia, as far back as 61,000 years ago, they wiped out the widespread and varied marsupial megafauna. They cite among others, the demise of animals such as the giant wombat, Diprotodon, the largest marsupial to ever exist. However, there is evidence accumulating that as in North America, these two events, the marsupial extinctions and the arrival of Australian aborigines, did not come close to occurring simultaneously. Australian megafauna became extinct between 46,000 BCE to 51,000 BCE. However, by some accounts, man has inhabited Australia as far back as 61,000 BCE. That would account for 10,000 to 15,000 years of human occupation in Australia before these animals went extinct. Once again, as in the North American situation, it is hard to understand why the Aborigines were able to coexist with the megafauna for such a long time and then suddenly developed methods and desire to wipe them out in a relatively short period. There is no evidence of a change in aboriginal technology at that time that might account for increased killing ability. It is important to note that like the Bushmen and Pygmies, the Australian Aborigines were Stone Age hunter-gatherers, who wandered on foot, in small groups of related people over a landscape that is mostly desert with a fragile ecology.

Australia is almost the size of the United States. No one knows for sure what the Aboriginal population was before the arrival of Europeans on that continent. The best estimate at the time of first contact between Aborigines and Europeans, in 1788, was 318,000 people. Australia has an area of 2,967,892 square miles. This would have averaged out to one Aborigine per 9.3 square miles. For comparison purposes, the least populous state in the

United States is Wyoming, which has 13 people per square mile. In other words, it would have taken 121 Aboriginal Australians to match Wyoming's present population density. Even assuming that Australia's population near the coast was larger than in its desert interior, it is hard for me to believe that such a tiny population, using Middle Paleolithic technology, could have killed off all of these large animals.

Massacre proponents, at first glance, appear to be on firmer ground when they cite what humans did in Polynesia. The accounts of Polynesian islanders wiping out many species on the islands they colonized are undoubtedly true. Nevertheless, this situation may not be relevant to the North American and Australian experiences. It is necessary to put these events in context by examining the special circumstances in which they occurred. Perhaps the differences that most distinguish the Polynesian experience is that these people were agriculturalists, not hunter-gatherers, and that they lived on islands. Their ancestors had migrated down into the Pacific islands from mainland Southeast Asia. Polynesians produced large amounts of food and stored it, thus enabling their populations to become much more dense than those of hunter-gatherers. However, this agricultural lifestyle also made them prone to population explosions, which put a strain on the carrying capacities of the islands they colonized. It was indeed their propensity to outgrow their islands' biological carrying capacities (the number of animals and plants that can be supported by a particular environment), that impelled their long voyages of discovery. The unique circumstance affecting the

Polynesians was their finite resources. Many of the islands on which they lived, were quite small, and when they had used up the local resources, they could not just pick up a few belongings and move to a more promising area as do contemporary hunter-gatherers, like the Hadza in Tanzania and the !Kung of the Kalahari Desert.

Human population pressures resulted in a kind of hopscotch invasion of more islands as the Polynesians pressed ever onward toward the Eastern Pacific, until they reached islands like Easter and Mangareva, which were distant from most of the other islands. The Polynesian's profligate ways led to starvation and sometimes their extinction when they continued them on such isolated, hard-to-get-to islands.

Easter Island is 3,000 miles from most other Polynesian-populated islands and archipelagoes (island groups). Despite the romantic notion that these Polynesian voyages were ones of exploration and adventure, it is not likely that such arduous and potentially dangerous journeys would have been undertaken except in a desperate search for new territory. These overcrowded conditions leading to heavy exploitation of their natural resources were among the primary factors in stimulating new voyages of discovery, as groups of marginalized or land-poor islanders searched for new islands to exploit.

Extinctions are more likely to occur on islands and happen more quickly on them than in other places. One of the main reasons for this is that once a faunal or floral population drops below a certain level, there is not much likelihood that they will be "rescued" by further in-migration. A present-day example of this condition is the predicament of wolves on Isle Royale. This is an island in Lake Superior to which wolves migrated, probably over the ice, during an unusually cold winter in the 1940s. Due to a variety of circumstances, the most important of which was that the number of wolves was never large, their population has recently crashed, and the wolves have become genetically inbred, showing severe and debilitating defects in their backbones. They are now in danger of becoming locally extinct. Scientists are debating whether or not they should import more wolves, thus effecting a "genetic rescue." They realize, however, that by doing so they would interfere with a valuable natural experiment, which they have been examining for more than 70 years. It will be a difficult choice to either watch the wolves probably go extinct or to taint the study by introducing "foreign" animals.

A well-known phenomenon known as "island dwarfism" occurs when many species isolated on islands become much smaller than their mainland relatives. A good example of this process, is the presence of dwarf rhinoceroses (*Dicerorhinus sumatrensis*) on the Indonesian island of Sumatra.

Island dwarfism may be due in part to the evolutionary pressures brought on by limited resources. Obviously, a smaller version of a rhinoceros or deer would have an advantage in such circumstances because they would need less energy to sustain themselves. This would be especially true of those animals living on islands in which their natural predators were never present or had been eliminated, so that their need to grow to a size large enough to defend themselves or flee predators was eliminated.

In perhaps another example of island dwarfism, Scientists have recently found fossils of diminutive hominids (human family members) only about 3 feet tall. Scientifically termed *Homo floresiensis*, these so-called "hobbits," were discovered in a cave on the island of Flores, also located in the Indonesian archipelago. These hominids resemble a smaller version of *Homo erectus*, a predecessor of modern humans, which to the best of our knowledge, became extinct some 400,000 years ago. An astonishing fact about these people is that one of the fossils has been reliably dated to 18,000 years ago. Perhaps it was their isolation on an island, separated by a deep, 50-mile wide trench from other islands in the archipelago that enabled them to survive almost to the present era.

Native inhabitants of Flores claim that these hominids are mentioned in their legends and that the accounts date back to the 1600s just before Europeans first visited the island. They call these beings the "little people" and say that they disappeared for good only after a volcano erupted near their cave. Wow! If their legends are true, and if that eruption had not taken place, we ourselves could have met a close relative of our ancestors. It is intriguing to contemplate such a near miss – not quite Jurassic Park but we would not have even needed to clone these people from fossil DNA.

An instance of a different effect of island isolation is the development of flightless birds on many islands, like the dodo (*Raphus cucullatus*) of Mauritius Island and the Guam rail (*Rallus owstoni*). From an evolutionary point of view, organs of flight are expendable if there are no predators to flee. Both of these birds are now extinct due to recent human predatory activities.

It is important to compare the Polynesian's ever-increasing populations with the stable condition of hunter-gatherer populations. Although we cannot be certain about the exact lifestyles of North America's Pleistocene hunters, we know from geographical, archaeological and DNA studies that their numbers were relatively small and sometimes led to the aforementioned population bottlenecks of only a few thousand souls. Small migrations that resulted in the peopling of large areas are not without precedent. The "Out of Africa" passage of *Homo sapiens* to the Near East and Eurasia around 60,000 years ago has been calculated by geneticists to have been made by only roughly 2,000 persons.

There is genetic evidence of at least two migrations, both small, from Siberia to North America, the earlier one eventually reaching South America and the later, larger one arriving in the northwest corner of the continent and spreading east and southeast to occupy what are now Alaska, Canada and the Lower 48.

We can also examine the populations and reproductive behavior of these North American migrants' present-day equivalents. Although they are scattered all over the world and usually have been forced into challenging and impoverished environments by tribal and Western technological cultures, hunter-gatherer cultures throughout the world are remarkably similar in many respects. Their populations, in contrast to those of agriculturalists such as the African Bantus, horticulturists such as the New Guinea highlanders, and migratory herders such as the Mosaic and Fulani in Africa, are remarkably stable, both between geographic areas and through the roughly 150 years in which they have been studied. Their groups usually consist of extended families of 10 to 30 persons who move from one area to another and back again, depending on season and availability of resources such as water, edible plants and game. Their numbers are self-limiting, due both to biological constraints and their use of a variety of birth control techniques. For example, in ways similar to the game they hunt, they reproduce more abundantly under ideal conditions and much less so under conditions of stress, such as lack of food and water. They also practice late marriage. For instance, among the !Kung (Namibian Bushmen), girls do not usually reach menarche (first menstrual cycle) and marry until their middle or late teens, while those of tribal agriculturists often marry even prior to puberty. Pygmies and Bushmen also breastfeed their children up to the ages of 4 or even later. Breast-feeding liberates hormones, such as oxytocin, that block ovulation. This is a natural method of birth control that has the effect of spacing children so widely that few hunter-gatherer mothers have more than three or four offspring. Contrast this with the families of agriculturalists, who often have as many as 10 children – the more the merrier. It takes lots of hands to run a farm, or at least it did until the advent of modern technology. Hunter-gatherers use other techniques to limit families, some of which are less palatable to our Western moralities. They use particular plants for their abortifacient qualities and have been known to leave newborns to die of exposure, when conditions are particularly desperate for them, choosing to try to save their other children and not add to the stress on them.

*A Hunter-Gatherer Job Interview – Gary Larson*

## The Climate Hypothesis

The alternative explanation for the Pleistocene extinctions, interestingly enough, is one that many people today still have difficulty in wrapping their minds around – climate change. In the present case, the reasons for denying the reality of these changes are clear enough. They are, first, that these have been mostly predictions of things yet to come and, secondly, accounts of some things that are happening now, not to us, but to other people. In an infamous remark while he was talking to James Hansen, one of the most renowned climate scientists in the world, well-known TV interviewer Larry King asked Hansen when some of these dire changes he warned of would occur. When Hansen told him that some would happen as soon as 50 years from now, King snorted, "No one gives a damn about what will happen 50 years from now." Lamentably, he was undoubtedly right. Humans have apparently evolved to react to present dangers, such as an attack from a saber-toothed tiger or an algebra test tomorrow morning, and not from future dangers that they may not be around to encounter.

In the case of the Pleistocene, at least, no one challenges the reality of these past climate changes, but frustratingly enough, the power of their effects are downgraded in the estimation of the massacre proponents.

## *The Beliefs of Earth-based Peoples*

I recall a story that Tom Brown told to my beginning survival class near the end of our course. Shortly after the birth of his first child, he took his son to a place in the Pine Barrens that held special significance to him, due to its beauty and the memories it held for Tom. He had intended to perform some sort of personal ceremony there to celebrate his son's birth, but when he arrived he discovered that the area had been turned into a dump. He told us that he placed his infant on top of the trash heap and had stood there weeping. There were few dry eyes in our class. I repeat this story because it illustrates the power of story to motivate people. I am sure that it has informed Tom's relentless entreaties to generations of his students to go out and save the earth. I know that it had that effect on me because I remember the story so vividly. Stories have real power, and that is why I believe those of Earth-based peoples have significance, even for us today.

Because of this, I present some additional evidence, in the form of stories and spiritual beliefs of Earth-centered peoples all around the world that I believe should be weighed in the extinction controversy. We have accumulated considerable knowledge about these beliefs, which indicate that North American hunters are not likely to have exterminated the megafauna.

I will begin with an Australian aboriginal legend called "The Kadimakara," as retold by Bruce Chatwin, a poet and naturalist:

According to the Aborigines, the desert they must cross to reach the oasis at Cullyamurra water hole was once a vast region of fertile plains and forests traversed by rivers flowing into lakes. The bones of ancient animals which we call diprotodons (note: the same ones the aborigines have been accused of exterminating) scattered en route were the surest proof that conditions had changed since that primordial moment. ... The present clear sky above had once been filled with dense clouds of dust, which perpetrated tropical downpours at regular intervals. Great gum trees reached high into the sky, supporting a complex interlace of green life that shut out all sunlight. From this arboreal vault, a group of monsters known as the Kadimakara descended in order to feed on the fruits below. Once these creatures had tasted the fruits of the Earth, their appetites became insatiable. In time they had eaten all the shrubs, trampled the Earth hard, and finally had resorted to eating the giant trees down which they had come. In an ironic twist of fate, they had destroyed their one escape route to the heavens! As a result, the Kadimakara were forced to remain on Earth. They wallowed in the lakes, drinking up the water. They ate everything before them. Soon the canopy of trees overhead had been destroyed, revealing one continuous hole of blue sky. The tribesmen named it Pura Walpinina, or the great hole. Meanwhile, the Kadimakara began to die of starvation now that they had eaten every shrub and bush. In the heaving marshlands of putrefying earth that had once been rivers and lakes, the monsters lay down to die. One by one they expired, their bodies slowly petrifying in the relentless sun, which their destruction of the natural environment had released upon the Earth. Their bones, the bones of the Kadimakara, littered the dry earth as somber reminders to the surviving tribesmen of what can happen when the natural environment is treated as an inexhaustible larder. The Kadimakaras' insatiable appetites had been the direct cause of their own extinction. Perhaps the aborigines were warning themselves that if they exceeded the carrying capacity of this fragile, barely livable area, they would suffer the fate of the Kadimakara. On the other hand, perhaps this cautionary tale is meant for ears other than those of aborigines who have lived in harmony with the Earth for so long. Perhaps this myth is of more recent origin, say since the days of first contact with Europeans and observation of their peculiar appetites.

Here is another story, from a very different place. This legend was told to James Cowan by an islander living in the Torres Strait, between New Guinea and Australia. His family was reputed by other natives to "own" the Pleiades (Seven Sisters) constellation. How can one own a constellation? Read on and find out:

> Tagai was a man. He owned a canoe, along with his friend, Kareg. One day they were out fishing with a crew made up of Usiam and Seg people. To you these people are the Seven Sisters and the stars in the belt of Orion. Anyway, while Tagai and Kareg were paddling along, the Usiam and Seg people decided to eat all the food and drink all the water on board. Kareg saw this happening and called out to Tagai, who was in the bow of the boat. So Tagai strung the Usiam together and tossed them in the sea. He did the same to the Seg people. Only Kareg, his friend, remained with him in the boat ... Yeah, the story of the stars belongs to me. I must interpret it for others, to remind them that all of us must take care not to act like the Usiam and Seg people. By drinking too much, by eating too much, we forget to leave some over for others. The food and water on Tagai's boat represents nature. If we use it up without thinking, we run the risk of exhausting our food supplies on the voyage.

Some people tell us that the only reason that American Indians and other indigenous peoples did not destroy their environments just as thoroughly as we seem on our way to doing, is that they lacked bulldozers and insecticides. I realize, of course, that it is in the nature of human beings to excel at finding reasons that reinforce their own beliefs, and that this propensity may even have evolutionary and survival value, by reinforcing their feelings of belonging to the group on which they depend. Nevertheless, I find it hard to believe that people whose stories show that regarded the rivers as their sisters, would have raped them by pouring toxic waste into them, or saw their forests as brothers, would have clear-cut them.

American Indians, who inhabited the Western plains, looked at wolves as older brothers and their scouts emulated them, like the Pawnee and Cheyenne did. Would such people have turned around and shot them from helicopters if only they had only possessed that equipment? Stories of traditional people, almost without exception, speak in the same moral tone, one of respect for their environment. They did not look at it as "an inexhaustible larder."

There is also anthropological evidence, accumulated from people whose behavior and customs most likely resemble that of our distant ancestors. Observations of contemporary hunter-gatherer groups show that they are remarkably like us. In fact, they are us. Biologically speaking, we are all still living in the Pleistocene. These people are certainly not Rousseau's "noble savages". They are capable of anger, envy, voraciousness and all the other dark emotions that people of our society exhibit. However, due to their relatively isolated environments and their needs, they have created lifestyles that discourage those darker behaviors and value many of the best human qualities, like cooperation, egalitarianism and community. These qualities have enabled them to tread lightly upon the

Earth and to live lives of integrity. I think that we still have much to learn from them.

## The Tale of the Blind Men and the Mammoth

Trophic cascades are ever-widening, usually top-down effects brought about by interactions between living organisms in ecosystems, particularly originating with predator/prey relationships. In these interactions, apex predators, like wolves and sharks, have profound effects on rest of their ecosystems, which like the proverbial pebble thrown into a pond, create ripples that reach distant shores. We are at present witnessing damaging cascades that are caused by a worldwide loss of top predators. This, in turn, is mostly due to human disruption of ecosystems, such as the effects of shark slaughter on fisheries.

William Ripple has traced trophic cascades in Yellowstone National Park from wolves to elk to willows and aspens, and to their widespread and important effects on the rest of the ecosystem. He showed in his studies that the explosion of the elk population, which occurred after the last wolves were exterminated in 1927, had deleterious effects that ranged from the disappearance of riparian flora to decreases in bird, fish and scavenger populations, and that the wolves, reintroduced in 1996, have been an important factor in restoring balance to the entire system.

Ripple also suspects that human predators may have been involved in the Pleistocene extinction of the woolly mammoth. He, and his colleague, Van Valkenburgh, presented intriguing evidence that mammoths may have fallen victim to trophic cascades some 10,000 years ago.

Ripple and his coworkers examined wear and fracture rates of Pleistocene fossil carnivore teeth from the Northwest in the United States. Heavily worn and fractured teeth are an indication of bone consumption, which predators avoid except when there is prey scarcity. They found that there was little indication of such wear. This evidence suggests that there were no serious food shortages in North America 10,000 to 15,000 years ago. Ripple believes that a range of predators, such as the dire wolf, lions and saber-toothed cats (*Smilodon sp.*) reduced the number of herbivores (plant eaters, mostly grazing animals). This ecological system was balanced but dominated by the predators. When humans arrived however, they may have tipped the delicate predator/prey balance, by providing increased competition for these predators.

Giving an example of a modern equivalent of this situation, Ripple said that in contemporary Alaska, human hunting of moose causes wolves to switch to sheep as prey, which in turn, results in a precipitous decline, not only of sheep, but eventually of wolves and moose, as farmers and their government proxies relentlessly kill off the wolves in retaliation. Ripple makes it clear that this contemporary trophic cascade started with that apex predator, man. Way back in the Pleistocene, predators desperate for food may have finally driven their prey to extinction. The authors argue by analogy that large reductions in whales due to human whale hunts have resulted in predatory Orcas (killer whales) switching to seals and sea otters as prey. This, in turn has led to an explosion in sea urchin populations and a decline in kelp forest ecosystems, in another example of a contemporary trophic cascade.

## *Dwindling Green Pastures*

Paleontology would not be paleontology, however, unless there were other researchers, who disagreed with Ripple. I found a rather convincing one. J.R.M. Allen, of Durham University, together with his colleagues, recently reported that a massive reduction in grasslands and the spread of northern forests may have been the ultimate cause of the Pleistocene decline in mammals. This reduction in plant life occurred during and after the height of the Ice Age, 21,000 years ago, and dramatically reduced available food for grazing animals. It resulted in the reduction of large mammals across northern Eurasia and North America by 11,400 years ago, although some held on for several thousand years longer in limited localities, termed "refugias," in which both climate and food supplies were more amenable to their survival. Migratory hunters were also restricted to refugias because of the availability of these mammals for their own food supply. Several of these areas have been identified, strung along the west coast of what is now called the Alaska Panhandle and British Columbia. Allen identified these environments, using ancient pollen records, and noted which major megafauna became extinct and which survived. The woolly mammoth, cave lion, giant deer, woolly rhino, and cave bear went extinct. The brown bear, elk, moose, reindeer, saiga antelope, and musk ox survived.

## *We Are All Connected*

Another scientist, D. Nogués-Bravo, has accomplished what amounts to a synthesis of the last two views. He used climate models and examined fossil distribution, concluding that change in global climate was accompanied by human pressures to drive the mammoths and other megafauna to extinction. Nogués-Bravo examined the possible effects in several climate models, ranging in age from 6,000 to 126,000 years ago. Clearly, the environment was much worse for mammoths 126,000 years ago, yet the animals survived. He showed though that there was a catastrophic loss of habitat 6,000 years ago so that only 10 percent of the former habitat remained. Nogués-Bravo also considered the effects of temperature changes and rainfall and then compared these parameters with age and distribution of fossils. He says that Arctic-adapted mammoths faced rising temperatures and increased hunting pressure at the same time. He argues that these animals had faced previous temperature increases without going extinct and the only difference was that this time there was human influence, so he came to the conclusion that it was a combination of climate change and human hunting that was responsible for these megafaunal extinctions.

Well, I have come to the place where I need to sum up the evidence and tell you of my conclusions. It turns out that it is not as easy to do as I first thought. I started out on this journey pretty sure of myself. I was on the side of the angels – at least they were my angels. I was pretty sure that the massacre proponents had at best exaggerated their case and at worst had become prisoners of their ideological propensities. However, Ripple, Nogués-Bravo and Allen have all impressed me, and also hopefully, yourselves, both with their novel approaches to the problem and their reasoned arguments. Nogués-Bravo and his colleagues particularly seem to have nicely combined Ripple's approach with that of Allen et al,

I do not think the last word has been said in this controversy by any means, but the idea that the demise of the megafauna was due, not to one, but to a combination of factors, including climate change and perhaps anthropogenic action, now seems more realistic to me than the either-or theories. Nevertheless, I still think that the preponderant evidence supports the idea that humans were not responsible, or played only a small role in the demise of these animals. If you disagree, I can only ask, "Vas you dere Charley"?

# Chapter Seven

# People of the Earth

$T$ypically, the avatars of Western culture do not put much stock in the legends, stories and myths of indigenous peoples. Being people of technology and the written word, we especially look down on those who have no written language, regarding them as "primitive" and therefore not worthy of being taken seriously, if we even bother to study them. Is there any validity, then, to the oral histories of indigenous peoples?

When we study another culture, we usually take only so-called hard evidence seriously. Evidence such as bones, implements, hieroglyphics$_2$ and ruins can be touched, photographed, categorized, and put in the form of graphs and tables. We even define whether a people had something called a "civilization" in such a way as to downgrade the importance of any people unless they had monumental ruins, a written (and decipherable) language, hierarchical social orders with division of labor, and whether or not they made war. (Guess which of the aforesaid counted highest?)

My point here, one that I have made in other places, is that I do not think that we attach sufficient significance to the beliefs of Earth-based peoples. Imagine if you can, that a future historian dismissed the Declaration of Independence and the U.S. Constitution as not having any bearing on the way people lived in North America during the past 200 years. I think that you would agree that such an attitude was ludicrous and showed sloppy scholarship indeed.

Yet, in a very real sense, this is what many scholars do when it comes to the beliefs and behavior of people whose traditions are oral. I believe that we should take these beliefs more seriously and give them more weight when we attempt to reconstruct events in pre-history. I came across the following story some years ago and found it to be a good example of this genre.

*Jon Young with Bushmen in Botswana – Jon Young*

## The Legend of Mount Mazama

This story comes from the Klamath tribe in Northern California and was told by a tribal elder to a soldier in

1865. Retold by Ella E. Clark in *Indian Legends of the Pacific Northwest*, Berkeley, University of California Press, 1952.

The story begins when the spirit of the Below-World fell in love with the chief's daughter and demanded that she marry him. This overture was denied and the rejection did not sit well with the spirit, who threatened to destroy the people.

"Raging and thundering, he rushed up through the opening and stood on top of the mountain."

The spirit of another great mountain now intervened and the two mountains began some sort of combat.

"Red hot rocks, as large as the hills hurtled through the skies. Burning ashes fell like rain. The chief of the Below-World spewed fire from his mouth. Like an ocean of flame, it devoured the forests on the mountain and in the valleys. On and on the curse of the fire swept, until it reached the homes of the people. Fleeing in terror before it, the people found refuge in the waters of Klamath Lake."

The Klamaths decided that someone should sacrifice themselves to appease the spirit. Two medicine men climbed the mountain and jumped into the opening.

"Once more the mountains shook. This time the chief of the Below-World was driven into his home, and the top of the mountain fell on him. When the morning sun arose, the high mountain was gone."

Then, according to the Klamaths, rain fell. For many years rain fell in torrents and filled the great hole that was made when the mountain fell.

This legend appears to be describing the simultaneous eruptions of two volcanoes. The very language seems to be evocative of volcanic eruptions. The Klamath's legend appears to be about Mount Mazama in Oregon and its twin, Mount Shasta in northern California, as having spirits who lived in them, and openings (vents and craters?) which led to a lower world through which the spirits passed. The Klamaths apparently knew when the mountain was active because when he (the spirit) came up from his lodge below, his tall form towered above the snow-capped peaks (smoke, steam?).

*Volcano Erupting – americanpreppersnetwork.com*

How would the Klamaths know about volcanic eruptions unless they had actually witnessed them? The only trouble with believing that this legend was a kind of transposition of an eyewitness account is that there had been no volcanic eruptions in the Pacific Northwest since Mount Mazama blew its top about 7,700 years ago and last erupted in 1,000 B.C.E. Mount St. Helens did not erupt until 1980, over a hundred years after the writing down of this tale. Could this story have been passed down from generation to generation for such a long time period?

Before you dismiss such an idea as fanciful, consider the part about the rain filling the great hole made when the mountain fell. It seems to be describing Crater Lake, which was formed in exactly that fashion when Mount Mazama collapsed.

*Crater Lake, Oregon – traveloregon.com*

Our culture, which depends on the written word and now also on electronic bytes, can hardly conceive of such prodigious feats of memory. However, many other cultures that depend on oral history to keep accounts of their people's stories have developed this capacity over millennia.

One startling example of this capacity is cited by anthropologist Wendy Doniger O'Flaherty in her delightful book, *Other Peoples' Myths*. O'Flaherty states: "India has two sorts of Sanskrit classics, typified by two great texts, the *Rig Veda* and the *Mahabharata*. The *Rig Veda* is a massive collection of hymns, a text of over 350,000 words (as long as *The Iliad* and *The Odyssey* combined); it was preserved orally for over three thousand years. The *Mahabharata* is one of the two great Sanskrit epics (the other being the *Ramayana*), a text of over 100,000 verses, or three million words (almost ten times as long as the *Rig Veda*, and fifteen times the combined length of the Hebrew Bible and the New Testament); it was preserved both orally and in manuscript form for over two thousand years."

These texts were recited flawlessly in villages from one end of the Indian subcontinent to the other without a single mistake. O'Flaherty tells the perhaps apocryphal story that it was only when these classics were translated by an English Consul into print that mistakes began to appear.

*Jeff King Sand Painting – britannica.com*

Navajo "singers" are capable of memorizing three-day ceremonies so flawlessly that no mistake creeps in. In fact, these ceremonies are never written down but are passed from one singer to another down through the generations. Joseph Campbell, the great mythologist, tells the amusing story of one such singer, Jeff King, who, in 1966, recited his ceremony and made a sand painting for a distinguished audience at the New York Museum of Natural History. When he had appeared to have finished, he was confronted by one very knowledgeable woman, who insisted that he had left something out.

"No," he said.

"Yes," she said, and insisted that he put it in.

"I cannot," he said. "If I did so, every woman in Manhattan would become pregnant."

As Campbell put it, "Those Navajo ceremonies had power!"

In sum, I believe that Western scientists and anthropologists are mistaken to dismiss the oral histories of these people. In doing so, they are losing a lot of valuable knowledge that may have at least as much validity as Carbon 14 isotope studies. The reason why I emphasize that oral histories should be taken more seriously is that I have trouble with people who tell me that the only reason that American Indians and other indigenous peoples did not destroy their environments just as thoroughly as we seem to be doing, is that they lacked bulldozers and insecticides.

*Wildlife Service Airplane Displaying Wolf Kill Decals -*
*APTASF*

# Chapter Eight

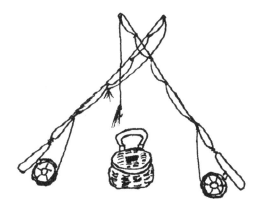

# The Fisherman
# And The Wolves

*T*he road down to the river looked so steep that I began to have misgivings about driving it. I tried to reassure my wife – and myself.

"It can't be this steep all the way," I told Lanie. "It leads to a fishing lodge. All kinds of dudes must go down here, including delivery and propane trucks. After all, we aren't exactly in the wilderness. We are only a few yards off of a highway."

Sure enough, the road soon flattened out and we came upon a cluster of log cabins and other wooden buildings. There was even a parking lot. We found ourselves on a sort of a shelf and we could see that the buildings below it were perched at various heights and strung along the side of a steep but short bluff above the Bull River. They were connected to each other by stairways and paths, and interspersed with immense ponderosa pines. Lanie was delighted with the sight and smell of these giant reddish-yellow trees, which exude a delightful odor of vanillin produced in their bark by the summer heat.

When we parked the car and got out, we could also smell pungent smoke curling up from a rooftop, indicating a wood fire somewhere ahead.

This place was beginning to look as advertised, a fishing lodge, albeit a rustic one. I liked the looks of it. I had never felt comfortable in fancy resorts. If they were half-timbered and had huge rock fireplaces and great views through the triangular windows under their eaves, I expected the owners of such places to be snooty and the prices for sleeping cabins and fishing guides to be sky high. This setup definitely looked to be our kind of place: slightly seedy, friendly-like and probably within our price range.

We descended on foot toward a weathered and ramshackle wooden building with a patched screened door and windows that appeared to have seen better days. This looked like it was the main lodge. On the way down we got a good look at the river, and by god it even had rapids! Rapids always excited me, a former whitewater kayaker. Some of my paddling buddies had bumper stickers that declared "we brake for rivers," and sure enough, Lanie and I almost always pulled our car over at bridges above creeks in order to "scout" rapids that we probably would never run.

Lanie and I were already quite familiar with the upper part of the Bull River. We had canoed it several times and even tried to fish it unsuccessfully. The parts we were familiar with were mostly as flat as a pancake and meandered gently around muddy banks and through grassy meadows. That section of the Bull also sometimes played peekaboo in and out of small patches of woods.

I had been told that the lowest three miles of the creek, just before it emptied into the much larger Clark Fork River, had Class III and IV rapids on it, but we had always taken our boats out well upstream from this more problematical section. Nevertheless, I was thrilled to see big rapids opposite the lodge. I thought, in my fishy naivety, that this is where the best trout would hang out, downstream of boulders and hiding beneath undercut banks. The fish would be delighting in the highly oxygenated whitewater and plentiful insect larvae that undoubtedly toppled off the river's banks and into their hungry jaws.

At least that was the tale I had read in all the books on fly-fishing I could devour. (At this beginning point of my fly-fishing career, I had ingested more written words than actual cutthroat trout.)

Looking back from my present vantage point in time and experience, it seems strange to me now that I had ignored the actual lessons that fishing the upper river should have taught me. The upper section looked like the exact opposite of what I thought a trout stream should be, as it meandered lazily through marshes and meadows. In fact, it hardly flowed at all, except during early snow runoff in the spring. Its bottom, which after that runoff was usually clear enough to see, appeared to consist of alternating sections of sand and silt, and was of a uniform depth except at the bends. In those places, the early spring currents had scooped it out and deepened it considerably, producing what fishermen and boaters call "holes."

That last point was important to me, because from what I could see, that was where most of the trout hung out, swimming around, sometimes as much as 10 feet down, near the bottom.

One time, while a gang of us was just canoeing down the Bull on a recreational trip, we had witnessed an insect hatch. This is the time that most fly fishers wait for and probably dream of because, as the insects land on the water surface, the trout consistently rise and gobble them up with an almost visible slurp. Oh, I thought, if we only had our fishing equipment with us! All that we would have had to do was to cast our dry flies on the surface of the water, and we would have caught so many trout that our arms would become weary!

Another time, spurred on by my previous discovery of these hordes of fish, I brought appropriate fly-fishing tackle along, determined to catch my supper. My fishing buddy, Mike, and I paddled lazily down the river, casting here and there, neither tempting nor even disturbing a single fish. The usual suspects were still there, milling around in the deep water at the river bends, and some of these trout looked huge. It was frustrating and somewhat humbling for us to be totally ignored by them.

Mike and I finally decided that if the mountain (or trout) would not come to Mohammed, Mohammed would go to the mountain, as the saying goes. We removed our dry flies and replaced them with nymphs (wet flies), which are weighted and sink down to the bottom. Then you pull them up, simulating the looks and action of hatching insects, and bam, you had a fish! Down went the nymphs, but the fish still paid no attention. It was maddening to the two of us.

I remembered another time when my wife and I were fishing up at the Old Man River in Crowsnest Pass, Alberta, with a friend from the Seattle area. Our companion was an accomplished fly fisher, having been introduced to the sport by her father when she was a young girl. On this day, she must have caught six fish for every one that I landed. We were all fishing the same spots, using the same kind of flies, but she really knew how to do it.

I studied her technique carefully, noting that it was

different from mine. I stood on the shore, making long, classically beautiful fly casts to the water near the far shore, and letting the fly float lazily down the river, next to the riverbank. She, on the other hand, waded into the river, cast her short line quickly into those same protected places, and when she did not get an instant strike, pulled her line out and cast again to a different place. In this way, she must have tried six casts to my every one and covered a lot more of the river. Maybe there was a connection. Six and six.

*Even I could catch a trout with a Royal Wulff Fly -*
*DryFlyOhio*

All right, I thought that day in Canada, if I cannot spot the fish, I should make many short casts to many likely spots, because if the fish did not respond immediately, it was either not there, or I did not "present" the fly in as lifelike a way as possible, or my karma was bad. If so, the fish obviously was not going to change its mind, so I might as well move on to the next one. This strategy worked, and I caught fish. Unfortunately, I growled to myself at the time, this river is "catch and release." Having to slip the fish off my barbless hook, and letting it fall back into the river was almost as painful to me as it was to them. I understand that the reason behind these regulations is to preserve fish for others to catch, but I still prefer "catch and eat." It seems to me that on these catch-and-release rivers, we were just hurting the fish for our own amusement, whereas our eating them would have served the higher, moral purpose of filling our bellies. Perhaps though, this point is debatable.

Later in my fishing education, I learned simply through observation that if you dropped your fly right in front of the trout's snout, it might just deign to take it. Trout, like most other wild animals, conserve their energy as much as possible, so they are not going to swim out of their way to check out a fly. That is also the reason why most of them lurk in eddies just downstream from rocks or beneath undercut banks where the current is slow.

It was obvious that we still had a lot to learn about fly-fishing, and that was the reason Lanie and I had just turned in at the fishing lodge sign.

On our way down the walkways we met several slim, young, athletic-looking men, wearing green or tan clothing, with lanyards around their necks dangling forceps, line cutters and a half dozen other indispensible fly-fishing paraphernalia. That, and the spare dry flies hooked onto foam inserts sticking out of their vest pockets definitely identified them as fishing guides. When we asked one of them where the owner was, he cheerfully pointed to one cabin where he said we would find Dave.

As I opened the rickety screen door, we were met by Dave himself, a smiling, rather overweight and jolly man, with a florid face and short-cropped grayish brown hair, who I judged to be in his 70s. When he rose to greet us, I noticed that he had a decided limp. He then sat himself back down in one of several holey, old upholstered armchairs grouped around a wood stove. Dave had a mug of coffee in his overlarge fist, and he offered some of the same to us. I gladly took one and we sat down next to large wooden table and talked about fishing and other fascinating things.

Dave told us that he had been a faculty member at the nearby university where he used to teach forestry. After he retired, he said, he had bought this lodge and set himself up in the fishing guide business.

"It's great to have the Clark Fork right at my door. It's got lots of big fish," he said.

He told us that he had arthritis (hence the limp), and for that reason he hired strong young men, who could row fishing dories down the river and haul them up on shore at the end of the day, while he took care of the business end and tended to his guests.

We chatted amiably about trout and where they could be found.

Then, we talked a little about costs at the lodge and for hiring a guide from him to go fishing. The guide service was, I thought, a bit pricey, but I knew already that was the usual case with fly-fishing. Because clients were typically affluent, the prices were tailored to their pocketbooks, and after all, it was one-on-one teaching.

Affluent we were not, so I calculated inwardly that Lanie and I might be able to afford one or two days of guided fishing, and that we could learn a great deal more about fly-fishing from this pleasant man and his assistants during that time. It sounded like we could have an enjoyable weekend at his lodge.

Dave regaled us with stories of places, such as Alaska, that he had been to, and fish that he had and had not caught. That prompted Lanie to ask:

"Have you ever been to the Frank Church River of No Return Wilderness?"

"No, I have not."

Dave's answer surprised me because the "Frank," as it is commonly called, is the largest wilderness area in the Lower 48 and occupies the entire middle of the state of Idaho, like a belt around a person's waist.

"Well, we once had jobs there with Idaho Fish and Game. We were caretakers and guides at their Stonebraker Ranch, in Chamberlain Basin," Lanie said.

She went on to explain what our jobs consisted of and that most of all, what we enjoyed about our summer in the wilderness was the abundant wildlife.

Dave was interested. He asked about the fishing in Chamberlain Creek and what wildlife we had encountered.

"Eagles, ospreys, elk, and moose, and oh," Lanie gushed, "we even heard wolves howling every night and early in the mornings."

Dave's demeanor instantly changed.

"Those goddamn wolves. They should kill every one of

them!"

Dave ejected this statement with a snarl. His face turned livid, his blue eyes narrowed and his forehead knotted. He was now audibly breathing almost in gasps as he wildly gesticulated (at the wolves?) outside the nearby window. "Wolves decimate elk, and they kill for pleasure. What good are they? The Feds should never have brought them here anyway. They're aliens and they're huge! They're over 200 pounds!"

Lanie stared at Dave with her mouth wide open in silent disbelief.

I, too, was shocked, but I jumped right into the verbal space between them, hoping to say something that would calm this unexpected storm. The change in mood of this hitherto jovial old man was so sudden that it was hard for me to think of how to react to it.

I thought to myself, Where did this venom come from?

I was used to hearing rants like this from wolf haters at Idaho Fish and Game meetings and had read many of them on anti-wolf blogs, but it was so unexpected from this nice man, and while we were his guests! How could I reply?

Then I thought, But this is a great opportunity! After all, I was Mr. Wolf Facts. I had learned so much about wolves and their real effects on the environment that I had been often tempted to reply to the angry and vituperative comments posted by badly informed people in reaction to newspaper articles and letters to the editor about wolves.

My few reasoned and fact-rich responses had invariably been met with so many more hate-filled and bizarrely inaccurate statements that I had soon given up on trying to reason with such people. That would be as much a waste of my energy as that of the fish who refused to check out my errantly cast fly.

But here was an opportunity to use my hard-gained knowledge of wolves in a more effective way. This man was an ex-college teacher. He must be used to hearing reasoned arguments and been trained to think critically and respect hard evidence. I would surely be able to reach him through the facts.

"So," I said, as calmly as I could, "that's remarkable. You might be interested in what Idaho Fish and Game learned about wolves from the first wolf hunt in that state in 2009."

Dave turned his head and stared at me intently as though he was just seeing me for the first time. The red color slowly faded from his cheeks and his breathing slowed to a more normal rhythm.

Seeing this change in him, I thought, Maybe I can get him to listen to me.

"Hunters killed about 188 wolves. They had to check the sex of each one of them and bring them to an Idaho Fish and Game station to register and weigh them. What Fish and Game found out was that the average female weighed about 87 pounds and the average male, 106 pounds. The largest male was about 126 pounds."

I waited expectantly for his response.

The florid color suddenly returned to Dave's face.

"Well, those were Idaho wolves. Montana wolves are different. They're huge!"

Now, it was my mouth that opened but no words came out. After a few more minutes of listening to his ever-escalating diatribe, I tried desperately to change the conversation back to safer topics, but Dave was having none of it.

"Those wolves are Canadian wolves and they're huge. They kill just for the fun of killing, and they're slaughtering all our cattle and sheep," he said, barely pausing for a breath. "And they have hookworm [tapeworm], and they've killed people up in Canada." I sighed, having heard all this too often before.

"Friends of mine are even afraid to leave their children at school bus stops because they've seen wolves around. The next thing you know, they're going to kill a child!" Lanie and I did not need to signal to each other. We mumbled something about being late to get home and extricated ourselves as gracefully as we could under the circumstances. We thanked Dave for his hospitality and even asked for a brochure in order to cover our hasty retreat. We quickly headed up the walkway, got into our Subaru and drove away.

When we reached the highway, we both sighed in relief. We felt as though we had escaped some awful fate, like being crushed by an inescapable landslide.

"What, if anything, have we learned from this?" Lanie asked.

"We learned not to talk with people we don't know about wolves," I grumbled..

As for the question as to whether our children are in danger of being devoured by wolves? I do not believe so, unless they wear red capes and sit in bus stops as illustrated on the next page:

# Chapter Nine

# My Son, The Indian

One of the saddest news items that I have seen in a long time, was that in which a reporter examined the impact of the Internet on kids. The response of one child who was asked why he spent most of his time indoors still haunts me. He replied, "Because that's where the wall sockets are where I can plug in my devices."

Most of us have heard about what Richard Louv, in his seminal book, *Last Child in the Woods*, calls "Nature Deficit Disorder." Louv says, "Our society is teaching young people to avoid direct experience in nature." More and more children and young adults are becoming dependent on their electronic devices that connect them to the Internet, and they are having less and less contact with the natural world. Psychologists and teachers are examining the effects that substituting a virtual world for the real one are having on those brought up and accustomed to relying on it.

It is worthwhile to consider this question from the point of view of evolutionary biology. Human beings are the product of millions of years of evolution, only roughly the last 5,000 of which have been spent under the influence of something we call civilization. Philosopher Paul Shepard emphasizes that we are living in a technological society, but we still have essentially Pleistocene bodies and minds. Continuing along this line of thought and his own observations, psychologist Erik Erikson, in his book

*Childhood and Society,* wrote about the crucial stages of development that all of us must pass through. Human development is a delayed one, compared with that of most animals, and many of its most important states occur not in the womb but in the years after birth. Most of us know this fact almost intuitively by having watched our own kids grow up and observing them stumble through the same passages of life we did, and which we call childhood, adolescence, young adulthood and so on. We try to mark some of the more obvious and important stages by celebrating them in various ways, such as bar mitzvahs, first communions, school graduations and so on.

Developmental psychologist Bill Plotkin, in his ground-breaking book, *Nature and the Human Soul,* which examines development from an ecological point of view, recognizes that many of the crucial stages are not the ones of physical growth such as puberty, but are also of psychological, emotional and spiritual development. Neuroscientists can even discern some of the anatomical and functional brain changes that take place in so-called normal development and what happens to the person when these changes are retarded, corrupted or do not happen at all. These stages do not occur and follow each other in a preordained way, like the ticking of an old-fashioned, windup a clock. They are mediated by our interactions with our environments and some of the most important ones occur through our experience with nature. For millions of years our ancestors were in constant and intimate contact with the natural world, and many of the events that triggered their maturation depended on their intimate relationship with it. What happens when that structure or framework is removed from our lives? As Joseph Campbell, the renowned scholar, once answered when asked about the effects of the loss of myth in our society, "Just look in the daily paper." (Or these days on the Eleven O'clock TV news).

Fortunately, there are those among us who are concerned about the effects of nature deprivation on our children and are trying in various ways to counteract this ominous trend. They have taken upon themselves the task of bringing our children back into connection with the natural world. I have had the privilege over the past couple of decades to come into personal contact with some of them and even to participate in their laudable and challenging undertakings. I would like to introduce you to a few of these people, in the hope that you will find their efforts both invigorating and inspiring. You will also see that they compose a cast of rollicking and colorful characters, who are willing to shoulder a burden that is perhaps too great for the rest of us to carry, but which is bringing about growth and great joy to many kids and a feeling of accomplishment and hope to their mentors.

## *"My Son, the Indian"*

"Take a look at this"!

Lanie was showing me a picture of a strange-looking dude on the front cover of one of those free weekly newspapers found in kiosks around New York City.

It was a head-and-shoulder shot of a person who looked like a mountain man. His broad forehead was topped by long, straggly blond hair that cascaded down his back to broad shoulders covered with a fringed, tanned buckskin shirt. The feature that struck me immediately were his strangely disconcerting eyes, wide open and impossibly blue. I was to become quite familiar with those eyes in the years ahead.

I thought to myself that this guy seemed like a combination of General George Custer and Peter Pan.

"His name is Tom Brown Jr., and he teaches courses in primitive survival," Lanie continued. "He says that you can go into the woods with nothing but a knife, and not only survive, but thrive there. I think that this is what I have been looking for my whole life. I would love to go into the woods without a huge backpack or a tent and all that other equipment people usually drag along with them. That 'stuff' just puts barriers between us and nature. I want to take Brown's course. It sounds exciting, and it's right near here, in the New Jersey Pine Barrens. You know, the place where we've gone canoeing. Will you come with me?"

I stared again at the picture. Brown looked to me like a crazy guy. I was to go into the forest with this nut and entrust my life to him? I knew enough though not to argue with the woman I loved whenever she decided to do some wild and crazy thing. I would either come along and watch over her, or she would go by herself. Well, this was the woman I had freely chosen as my life companion, right?

I first met Lanie at a Halloween party back in the 1980s. We both got a lift home from Brooklyn to Manhattan in the same car, and on our way late that night, she opened the car door when it stopped at a red light on the corner of 8th Avenue and 14th Street, bounced out, and airily announced to the driver: "You don't need to turn here. I'll walk home the rest of the way."

In lower Manhattan – at 3 in the morning – she was going walk six blocks by herself?

Before we had time to remonstrate with her, off she went.

Hmm, I thought, an interesting woman!

The following morning, wasting no time, I telephoned my kayaking buddy, Karl, who had hosted the party and asked him to get me her telephone number.

Thus began a seemingly endless series of adventures with Lanie. On our first date, we ended up sneaking into a labyrinthine religious seminary, plumb in the middle of Manhattan, and slipped through all kinds of twisting, winding passages and back stairways that were probably unfamiliar, even to most of the seminarians.

Then, there was our first trip to Princeton University, which I had naively thought was for the purpose of meeting her father, who was a biochemistry professor there. Well, it was, kind of, but how did she inveigle me to climb nine flights of stairs in the McCarter Theater across the street from the house in which she grew up, and then open an unobtrusive metal hatch in a dressing room wall, and slide down nine floors on an enclosed and pitch-black stainless steel helical fire escape chute until we popped out of a similar hatch outside the ground floor?

It was lucky that her father did not catch us as he had done with her when she was a 10-year-old tomboy. What a great impression Dr. Fischman would have made on his prospective father-in-law!

Then, of course there were all the brambles she led me

into on hikes into the New Jersey's Great Swamp and the Shawangunk Mountains in upper New York state, where she stubbornly resisted staying on the well-marked trails.

"Oh, well," I sighed yet again, resigned to the prospect of rambling down another of her bramble patches.

We ended up spending a week taking Tom Brown's Standard Survival course in the Pine Barrens, a huge, almost-trackless semi-wilderness area tucked into the southeastern part of the New Jersey. It is a place unknown to most of the people who go zipping right by it on the bustling New Jersey Turnpike. We learned (somewhat) how to make fire without matches by making and using a bow drill, to do rudimentary tracking, and dozens of other useful and fun survival skills.

Most impressive, we witnessed the uncanny and apparently superhuman abilities of a master survivalist. One time, our class was standing on the shore of a pond, waiting 10 minutes impatiently for Tom to show up, when he suddenly popped up in the middle of it, dripping wet, and with weeds and tangled grass on his head. He had been there all the time, watching us. On another occasion, 50 students, including yours truly, who were ostensibly studying awareness as the most valuable of all wilderness skills, walked down a woodland path to our dinner spot, and none of us noticed Tom lying in the grass not more than two feet off the path. These feats were explainable as those of a master of camouflage, but some of his other abilities defied easy analysis.

Tom Brown made the woods and the art of primitive survival come alive for the two of us. We yearned to put ourselves to the test and try some of these skills out. And try them out we did, even though we were living in Manhattan, New York City, one of the most densely populated urban areas in the country. We camped without a tent that summer in northern New Jersey's mosquito-infested Great Swamp, and that winter we tracked weasels and pheasants in the snow in Manhattan's Central and Inwood parks. We were hooked on primitive skills.

The following year, we took Tom's second course, the Advanced Standard, given at an old farm on the banks of New Jersey's Musconetcong River. There, we learned how to build survival shelters, flint knapping (fashioning stone tools and weapons), pottery making, gathering wild food plants, and many wilderness awareness skills, such as becoming invisible to animals. Most of the time we learned these skills by doing them, but part of each day, we sat on the floor of a rickety, two-story barn and listened to lectures and stories from the most charismatic teacher I have ever encountered. One day, Tom strode into the barn, late as usual. His staff called this "Tom Brown Time."

We, his students, were already assembled, waiting for Tom. He looked at us, mounted the podium ready to give his lecture, and then seemed to hesitate. An amused smile crept over his ruddy face.

"Who's been up in the rafters?"

Silence reigned.

"Come on, you're not going to be punished. Who's been up there?"

He had not so much as glanced upward.

Finally, a blonde, buxom young woman, attired in shorts and a tank top, rose hesitantly in the back of the barn.

Shamefaced, she said: "I was up there. I wanted to see if you would become aware of me. You talk so much about awareness, but I chickened out."

"How did you know that she had been up there?" asked a tall, skinny young man wearing a white T-shirt.

"It was the barn swallows," Tom replied. "They weren't singing. They are always up there."

We glanced up at the rafters. No swallows.

This was my first inkling of Tom Brown's almost otherworldly awareness abilities, that and the almost constant lateral oscillations of those piercing blue eyes. At first, I thought that he had nystagmus, a congenital or inherited vision defect, in which the eyes are never still. Later though, I discovered that he was in what he called "splatter vision" mode, a kind of wide-angle vision that wild animals use to detect motion in a more than 180 degree field around them. It was a valuable survival skill, especially when your life depends on instantly spotting a predator creeping up on you. Next time you watch a deer browsing, notice that its eyes are constantly moving as it picks its head up every few seconds. No wonder deer are hard to sneak up on, but Tom and some of his advanced students have actually been able to stalk close enough to a deer to touch it! However, that is a story for another time.

You have to know something about Tom's childhood to appreciate how he gained these abilities. Tom Brown's life reads like an improbable story but apparently is true. As a 7-year-old kid, he met his best friend Rick's grandfather, who turned out to be an elder in a Lipan Apache band from the Southwest who used to be a scout for his tribe. Tom and Rick spent almost every spare moment with

Grandfather up to the age of 15, learning American Indian lore, skills and philosophy in the nearby Pine Barrens. You can read about his sometimes rollicking, sometime frightening, but always fascinating adventures, in Tom's book, *The Tracker*. Tom spent so much of his time surviving in the Barrens that once his father, a clergyman, spotting him reentering the house after one of his ventures, sighed,

"There goes my son, the Indian."

By my calculation, Tom Brown has taught well over 50,000 people how to survive in the woods and imbued many of them with a fire in their bellies to go out and help save the natural world. Not bad for a backwoods redneck, who still personally teaches every class in the "Tom Brown Tracker School."

### The Talking Gorilla

During this time in the '80s, when Lanie and I were taking many Tom Brown classes, I came across a curious little book entitled *Ishmael*, which was written by Daniel Quinn. Quinn is an elfin little man, with a constant twinkle in his eyes, who has an alternative view of the culture in which we live. Did you ever read a book that changed your entire outlook on life? Ishmael was that kind of book for me.

Did you ever have a dream that haunted you for years, trying to puzzle out its meaning? Of course, some people, like Ebenezer Scrooge in Dickens' *A Christmas Carol*, and various neuroscientists, do not believe that dreams have any particular meaning. Scrooge, when confronted with the ghost of his former partner, Jacob Marley, tried to allay his fear by attributing this frightening vision to "a piece of undigested mutton."

"This strikes me more of gravy than of the grave," he said.

Some scientists, however, take a more, well, scientific approach, attributing dreams to pieces of undigested ideas floating around in our minds and put together in the form of a story at the insistence of those selfsame minds.

My bias on this subject runs in the opposite direction, due to my own experiences with both troubling and recurring dreams that I felt revealed some important truths to me.

I am pretty sure that Daniel would agree with me because he had a dream at the age of 7 that changed his entire life. In that dream, he was walking at night on the sidewalk next to a stone wall surrounding a large, wooded park. He came upon a huge, overturned tree that blocked his path. He was trying to slip through the twisted branches and over the trunk to the other side when he was confronted by an enormous black beetle as large as himself. Seeing his fright, the beetle reassured him that it meant no harm but had only made the tree fall so that it could warn him that the beetle and all of the other denizens of the woods were in mortal danger and needed his help.

Quinn never forgot this dream, and some 50 years later created a talking gorilla in place of that beetle, as the hero of his Ted Turner prize-winning book, *Ishmael*. That gorilla talked incessantly, essentially warning mankind through the many entertaining stories he told that the way that its present culture was constructed was leading mankind on the path of self-destruction and was dragging the rest of the community of life along with it.

Without gorilla will there be hope for man?

Ishmael
by Daniel Quinn

*Quinn's Narrator, Ishmael – Daniel Quinn*

Ishmael was a transformative book for me. I will never see the world in the same way after reading it. Most importantly, it informs us about a culture that preceded that of our own and still exists in hidden and remote places, one that found a way to live in harmony with the rest of the world. The hunter-gatherer culture is one that we have all but obliterated and forgotten, but its continued existence puts to the lie the idea that ours is the only culture in which man can live, is the perfect way to live, and yet which many of our religious tomes insist is unalterably flawed. Are we flawed in our very essence? If so, why try to make things better if what we are and what we produce is inevitably and totally the product of our innate human nature? Quinn poses a simple question: Is the butterfly flawed, is a bacterium flawed, is the lion flawed? Then, why are we the only imperfect creature in the universe? His answer, rejecting the biblical tale of our expulsion from the Garden of Eden, is a renunciation of the old nature-versus-nurture argument. He says that human behavior is the result of the interaction between both our inherent nature and the environment in which we find ourselves – and increasingly the one that we ourselves create.

Quinn makes the point that if hunter-gatherers like the Bushmen of South Africa, the S'Nng hoi of Malaysia, the Hadza of East Africa and many others, now hidden away in the secret corners of the earth, can create cultures that are at peace with the world, then we, too, can find our own way to that end. Why not? We are a marvelously inventive species. If I did not believe this, I would not waste my time writing this story. I would instead go out and play golf.

## Back to the Pleistocene

The first time I attended the Rabbitstick Primitive Skills rendezvous, when I pulled my truck camper into Dave Wescott's ranch in Rexburg, the thought struck me that I had driven not only to southeast Idaho but back deep into our continent's past. The partially treed meadow, bordering a bend of the Henry's Fork River, was alive with a strange mixture of oddly dressed people and even odder-looking dwellings. Most of these lodgings were Plains Indian tepees of various sizes, some colorfully decorated and others made of plain white canvas (bison hides are scarce these days). There were other temporary dwellings, too. Some of them looked like huge white umbrellas with their poles stuck into the ground at an angle so that they leaned toward the southwest, and they were secured by lines tied from the ends of their ribs to wooden stakes driven into the ground. These strange contrivances were actually surplus parachutes that were being used as work areas protected from the sun and rain; they were called "jellyfish" due to their fancied resemblance to those membranous marine creatures.

*Rabbitstick Encampment – Ken Fischman*

This similarity was especially striking when the wind rippled their sides, like currents do to their namesakes. There were also white canvas tents, cubical in shape, with peaked tops, reminiscent of outfitters' tents. In fact, that was exactly what they were. There were a scattering of more contemporary-looking, one- and two-person tents, mostly tucked into the edges of the surrounding woods, and a few monstrous RVs that looked incongruous in that setting.

A tall, angular, brown-eyed man, wearing a beige Stetson cowboy hat, greeted us at the registration tent. He looked like he had just stepped out of an old Hopalong Cassidy or Gene Autry film. He had a handlebar mustache and was wearing tight blue jeans, cinched with a silver buckle belt, and topped with a red-checkered shirt, blue-and-white kerchief, and a brown leather vest. He, of course, was wearing embossed cowboy boots.

*Dave Wescott – Ken Fischman*

*Women in charge of the Rabbitstick Children's Program –*
*Ken Fischman*

Lest you think that this primitive skills camp is like the various "mountain man rendezvous" that take place in the United States and Canada, there are some stark differences. First of all, mountain man rendezvous are costumed period pieces, actually reenactments of a time in North America when adventurers and fur trappers first invaded this continent. After a winter of hard work and discontent, they would gather in various "holes," or valleys out West, and have a rendezvous, during which there would be much singing, dancing, trading of goods and carousing. Actually, from what I have read, the carousing part was their major function. Naturally, in such circumstances and being a gathering of such rough men, there was usually a problem of preventing the whole shebang from blowing up in mayhem. They solved this problem by appointing a man called a "bourgeois," who posted long lists of rules and had the authority to enforce them, sometimes in an equally rough way.

In Rabbitstick, all of these cumbersome rules and enforcements were avoided by the enactment of one simple rule, which was shouted by all in our answer to Dave's first question at our first get-together in each year's encampment.

"What is the Law of Rabbitstick?" Dave would yell, and the answer would come reverberating back from the rest of us.

"Stupid people die."

We then went peacefully about our business for the rest of the week.

There are many technical types involved in Rabbitstick activities, given that most of the skills of primitive living and techniques for creating primitive tools have had to be reinvented because people of our time had only the faintest idea of how to make them. For example, flint knapping, the art of fashioning stone tools and weapons, was lost knowledge, unknown to us until a couple of decades ago. People had been digging up arrowheads, stone axes and other such implements for centuries, but they had been unable to duplicate them. A lot of trial-and-error went into the first efforts to reproduce these objects, and engineer types were very useful for such purposes. For example, they had to find out what sorts of rocks, such as chert and obsidian (volcanic glass), lent themselves to these techniques and how they could be fashioned. Some of these people experimented with heating these rocks and found out that it sometimes changed their crystalline structures, thus making it easier to fashion them into usable tools.

Some of the weapons used by our ancestors, such as bows and arrows, are familiar to us, but others are not. A few years ago, I learned how to make a spear thrower, or atlatl, from an expert at Rabbitstick. Atlatls harness the power of physical principles by utilizing a notched stick, holding in place a javelin or short spear, thus extending the length of your throwing arm artificially. This extra length can enable even me to hurl a javelin the span of a football field with great power and accuracy into the side of a gazelle. (I just use targets. No gazelles were hurt in the making of this story.)

Lest you get the idea that Society of Primitive Technology (SPT) is just a group of people who sit around all day chipping away at rocks, I assure you that is only one small aspect of the rendezvous. Above all, Rabbitstick is a place for learning. The experts who teach classes there come to it not only from all over the United States and Canada but also from Europe, South America and other parts of the world. A fee for coming to the rendezvous covers the cost of two meals a day and use of facilities. Beyond that initial charge, most of their classes are free.

Just a few teachers charge extra for materials such as tanned hides, beads, etc.

The camp was set up in a well-organized fashion. Dwellings were here, the kitchen there, port-a-potties someplace else, and the arrow and spear targets in back, away from everything else. The flint knapping pit was situated all by itself at the far end of the camp, where barefoot kids would not be likely to stray and have the soles of their feet cut up by discarded razor-sharp rock fragments.

Interestingly enough, the entire setup reminded me of an article I read about a primitive hunting camp that paleontologists had recently discovered in east Germany at Bilzingsleben. Again, the garbage pit was at one end of the camp and the flint knapping pit at the other – very organized and efficient. The only disconcerting thought about it was the age of that camp: 400,000 years. How could our distant ancestor, *Homo erectus*, who constructed that camp, have learned these things? Were such beings capable of learning, forethought and planning? Perhaps they had attended a Rabbitstick Rendezvous.

One of the first things I do when I arrive at Rabbitstick is to head for the bulletin board, which is covered with notices about the courses that are being given. The assortment is bewildering and almost overwhelming in number and diversity. It looks more like a menu in a Chinese restaurant than a curriculum. You know, one from column A and another from column B and so on. I find that the immediate challenge I face is in deciding which classes I am yearning to take that do not overlap or coincide with others that I also desperately want to participate in.

*This year*, I thought, *I will take the class in bow making, offered by a master bowyer (or bow maker), or do I prefer the one in how to make pigments and dyes from natural materials like mushrooms, fungi, bark and so on? How about taking the class in foraging for wild foods and basket making materials from a renowned botanist, Dr. John Kallas?*

John is pretty far out. He has done such outrageous things as tasting a water hemlock. He had read in several manuals that the water hemlock (*Cicuta maculata*), a deadly poisonous plant responsible for many deaths, has a bitter taste. Why, then, would anyone eat it? he reasoned? In order to determine the truth, he chewed up a tiny piece and then spat it out. He found it to be sweet, but his lips and tongue lost their sensitivity for several minutes. I was content to take his word for it instead of personally checking it out.

In the last Rabbitstick I attended, I decided to go into a nearby marsh with a botanist who specializes in wild food and learn how to harvest and process cattail plants (*Typha angustifolia* or *latifolia*).

Tom Brown calls these rushes "the supermarket of the swamps," and with good reason. If you are ever lost in a swamp or marsh, you do not have to starve. Different parts of the cattail are packed with nourishing food. That botanist showed us how nutrition-rich its underwater roots or rhizomes were, and how they can either be roasted or pounded into flour. We also discovered that the shoots at the ends of the roots are delicious if harvested in the right season, and that they can also be eaten raw. Cattail pollen, from the tassel at the top of the plant, can also be used for flour, and the green flower heads can be boiled and eaten. We tried all these methods and had a big plant feast. If that is not enough for one plant's utility, you can also weave its long, broad leaves into useful products, too. Sunshades, anyone?

*Cattails at Rabbitstick – Ken Fischman*

And then there is Cody Lundin, the barefoot desert survival teacher! There are a lot of colorful characters who show up at Rabbitstick, but Cody gets my vote for the most unique figure. He is hard to miss. With his muscular and scantily dressed body, he looks like a professional wrestler. His sloping, powerful shoulders have either developed from hours of practicing hand-drill fire starting or perhaps they are just natural and have made him a master of that art. Square-jawed and with long, flaxen hair kept in twin, braided pigtails and topped by a red or blue bandana, Cody and his baby-blue eyes, smile and always-pleasant disposition are a familiar sight at our rendezvous. He always seems to be surrounded by a bevy of young women. I do not know why.

*Cody Lundin – Cody Lundin*

His most outstanding physical characteristic though is his feet. (Sorry, you guessed wrong, ladies). Always barefooted, he has developed thick calluses on them from wandering for many years without shoes through thorny cacti in the Sonoran Desert. The most famous story about Cody is that that Walmart will not allow him in their stores due to his naked tootsies, and he swears to never set foot in one until they change their policy. This struggle between the man-child and the massive corporation has reached a deadlock, with Cody trashing Walmart at every chance he gets in his classes.

Lundin's survival school is quartered somewhere out in the desert near Prescott, Arizona. Cody's philosophy, delightfully laid out in his survival manual, entitled *98.6 Degrees: The Art of Keeping Your Ass Alive*, is seemingly at odds with that of Tom Brown, who preaches primitive survival and whose idea is that you can go naked into the wilderness and do just fine. Although Cody probably endorses the naked part, he believes that you should use any man-made material available to help you survive, and in being prepared by taking survival kits wherever you go. His idea of what should go into those kits is rather idiosyncratic, ranging from Vaseline-coated, gasoline-soaked cotton balls for getting fires started to carrying Trojan brand condoms as emergency and compact water containers. Although I appreciate the sheer ingeniousness of this last item, I have always suspected that he might have had other emergencies in mind, too. After all, you never know what you will bump into during desert excursions.

Lanie and I went to these shindigs for more years than I want to think about and loved every minute, learning and teaching, visiting with old friends, and wondering if way back when, this was how functional communities were formed. If so, I want to go back there.

## *Honoring a Great Man*

I was suddenly wide-awake at 3 a.m. My inner alarm clock had gone off, but I was not accustomed to waking this early. I actually hate getting up in the middle of the night and usually could be forced to do it only if I had to drive to the Spokane Airport in order to catch an early morning plane. I was groggy and ill tempered, but I remembered that I was on a mission. I wanted to get over to the nearby Twin Eagles Wilderness School before dawn.

I hastily pulled on my longies and other cold-weather clothing. It was late fall, and I anticipated that it would be cold outside in the pre-dawn. I stumbled around in the kitchen, making some hot herbal tea, and poured it into two steel thermos bottles that I had just heated with boiling water. That would keep them hot for several hours. I walked outside into the darkness of northern Idaho. Innumerable white stars twinkled against the blue-black sky above me, and I recognized an old friend up there, the constellation, Orion, The Hunter. I shivered. It was colder than I even expected, undoubtedly due to the clear night sky sucking up heat from the ground.

A 20-minute car ride later, I arrived at Twin Eagles. I parked my Subaru Outback and walked as quietly as possible into the woods in back of Jeannine and Tim's large, yurt-like but stick-built house. I did not want to wake up either her or her young children, River and Forest. All around me, the mixed pine, cedar and fir forest was still silent.

The ground crunched beneath my feet because the grass was stiff with early morning frost. I could smell the fragrant lodgepole pine wood fire, and its increasingly strong scent guided me to where Tim was camping. Sure enough, there was the fire, just winking out into orange coals, and Tim was asleep on the ground alongside it in his sleeping bag, which was covered with a blue, plastic tarp to keep out the dew.

As quietly as possible, I gathered some of the smaller pieces of wood from the pile that Tim had placed within easy arm reach, and carefully stacked them on the dying embers. I blew on the cinders gently but steadily for a few minutes until they burst into flame and engulfed the wood.

I sat down on a rough pine log where I could be comfortable and able to continue feeding the growing fire from time to time. When I finished my task, I looked up and could see a faint but glowing light in the east above the tops of the trees surrounding us. Dawn was coming. I opened my thermos and sipped some of the hot tea. My, I thought, how good it is and how strangely peaceful I feel on this sad night.

Tim stirred and awakened. He looked up and seemed surprised and pleased to see me there. We hugged. He got up, stretched and headed for the house to say good morning to his family.

I knew that all over this country, Canada and in other parts of the world, special fires like this one were burning today as the dawns crept up. This was the way, in so many parts of the world, that Earth-based peoples and those of us who admire their traditions and rituals mark the death of a great person.

As one of the heads of Twin Eagles, a school dedicated to bringing children back into connection with Earth, Tim had taken this task of tending the fire all night as his way of honoring Jake Swamp.

Jake Swamp, what a humble name for an unobtrusive, little man who had such personal power. Jake Swamp was the Peacemaker of the United Iroquois Tribes, whose members lived in the upper northeast region of what is now the United States and Quebec.

How can I describe him? While he lived, if you had crossed his path on a crowded city street, you probably would not have given him a second glance. There was nothing extraordinary looking about Jake. He was short of stature, smooth complexioned and had gentle, brown eyes and sparse brown hair. He seemed to walk as if not to disturb anybody or anything. You would not know how extraordinary he was unless you sat opposite him for a while and listened to what he had to say.

It was not always thus with Jake. To hear him tell the story, he had been quite a hell raiser as a kid and young man on the Mohawk tribal reservation in upper New York State, always in trouble. In our culture, we would have thrown someone like Jake away, put him in jail and forgotten about him, but not the elders of Jake's tribe. They constantly harassed him, challenged him, and made him pay in service and humbleness for every one of his transgressions, but they would not disown him. It was not their way. They saw the power in him even then, and they nourished it, in much the same manner in which I had just reawakened the flames of his funeral pyre, with patience, toughness and understanding. He grew to be the humble man who addressed legislatures and the General Assembly of the United Nations and started a movement that had grown worldwide, to teach the rest of us the American Indian ceremony of giving thanks to the Earth for our lives. The full version of this thanksgiving could go on for quite some time because there were a lot of entities to thank, but it weaves a spell, and at the end, when we are asked to "bring our hearts and minds together." We really are all on the same wavelength.

Tim had returned by now. I gave him the other thermos, and he sipped it. He let me know again how much he appreciated my presence at such a time. We sat there and talked about Jake and the effects that he had on our lives.

Tim went back quite a ways with Jake, but me, not so much. I remember the first time I met him, only a few years ago, when he came to Sandpoint. He spoke for two days at a rustic, outdoor amphitheater adjacent to a small Forest Service campground. And what did he talk about?

He told us a story. This is the way those American Indians who cling to their traditions pass important information on to others. Jake told us about the Iroquois Peacemaker. I cannot possibly do his story justice by trying to repeat it. In fact, on the second day of his talk, he laughingly told us: "If you think that this is a long story, you do not know the half of it. I am giving you a shortened version. When I tell it to tribal people, it takes a whole week."

American Indian meetings and stories are often eye-rollingly long to the unpracticed ears of us outsiders. They go on and on and on until everybody gets it and is on the same bandwidth.

The Peacemaker is an Iroquois legend, and I can only give you a bare outline of it. To try to do more would be like attempting to recite the Odyssey at one sitting.

In short, these six, now united tribes, were for a long time continually at war with one another, and much blood had been shed. But, one time, long ago, rumors began to spread among them that there was a Peacemaker, who lived deep in the swamps of the wilderness, and he was coming to talk with them. His coming was a long one, and he had to employ every bit of his shrewdness and street smarts just to not get killed by these warring tribesmen before he even reached the first village. These tribes hated each other and feared all strangers, and for good reason, if you knew the mayhem they had done to each other.

As we listened to Jake tell the tale, it gradually became clear that we were not only listening to an enchanting story, but he was laying out a blueprint for his listeners on how to bring about peace between warring parties. No wonder he spoke at the U.N. General Assembly. He had a lot to teach them.

Just a few tidbits: The last tribe the Peacemaker contacted was the worst. It was feared by all the others, and was ruled by a cannibal king. After pacifying him, no easy task in itself, the Peacemaker put him in charge of restraining the tribes' internecine warfare. Needless to say, the warfare stopped like magic.

Tim remembered especially when Jake told us that in order to become a peacemaker, you first had to find peace within yourself. You cannot convince others unless you can talk out of authenticity. That would be the biggest challenge for anyone wishing to follow in his tracks.

My favorite part of the Peacemaker's story is his giving the grandmothers of the United Tribes veto power over the decision to go to war. They have not had a war since.

## *Tom Brown, Shaman?*

One of the things that I love about Tom Brown was the way in which he stretches the sense of what our minds could do. For example, one day during our second class with him, the Advanced Standard, he explained to us that we could visualize ourselves as scouts and send them out to a place we could not see in order to reconnoiter it for us. Since I am essentially lazy, this technique certainly appealed to me. If I were tired, I could simply send out my scout to check out what was down the trail. I thought that this would be especially valuable to me as a whitewater kayaker who often felt anxious about what he might find in that rapid ahead that he could not see but could hear around the bend. It would have been really nice to know where the holes and rocks were before I committed myself to running it.

I was already familiar with Tom's concept from my childhood listening to the radio program, "The Shadow," which dealt with an invisible man. Lamont Cranston, man about town, was able to pull this stunt off because, "Years ago in the Orient, he had been given the power to cloud men's minds." Cranston, aka The Shadow, was also given to such sage remarks as "Who knows what evil lurks in the hearts of men. The Shadow knows!"

Of course, as an adult, I did not believe in such stuff any more, so I looked askance when Tom told us to go out and test our new powers by meditating, and then sending out our scouts to check something in a place we had never been. Then, he said, we should go to that place and "prove it."

I had great doubts about the efficacy of his method but was still willing to keep an open mind and try it. Oh well, I thought to myself, as a scientist, I was trained to test things out no matter what my biases, and this sounded like an easy-enough task. I wandered out of our Pine Barrens camp and soon found myself in an area I had never been to previously. I saw a sand ditch there, one of many that had been dug as a firebreak to hinder the numerous conflagrations that erupted in the barrens during hot summers. I sat down on the bank of one ditch and went through the meditative procedure that Tom had taught us. I especially remembered the part of it where Tom, frustrated with our slowness in picking it up, shouted, "Relax, damn it!"

That sure helped.

I sent my "scout," whom I named "Ken Pathfinder," ahead, around a corner of the firebreak. I mentally inserted myself in this scout and imagined myself looking out through his? her? its? eyes. I was peering down a long trail and clearly saw some canine tracks crossing it about 50 feet ahead.

This is ridiculous, the real me said to myself. First of all, we have not seen or heard any of the infamous Pine Barrens dogs around the entire week that we have been here, and besides, it rained heavily last night. Even if there had been such tracks, they would surely be erased from the sandy soil by now.

I got up, walked around the bend and stared down a

surprisingly familiar and straight section. I walked about 50 feet, eyes glued to the soft, wet sand track, seeing no tracks. Then, I came to a large tree trunk, recently fallen across the ditch. "

I am not going any farther. No tracks, I thought, with satisfaction. I told you so.

Then, I happened to glance beneath the trunk, and there in the sand was a perfect canid paw print. When I got over my shock, I tried to figure out what had happened. A dog had loped across the ditch, perhaps as far back as two weeks ago, and shortly afterward the tree had fallen across the ditch, thus protecting the track from being erased by the rain or eroded by the wind.

Now I was at war with myself. Of course the "objective" scientist in me dismissed this episode as mere coincidence, yet I could not adequately explain the incident in a rational way.

A few years later, I was reading Laurens van der Post's book, the *Lost World of the Kalahari*, which details his post World War II expedition to find the last remaining South African Bushmen, when I came across the following anecdote. With game very scarce around the bushmen's camp, van der Post drove some of the hunters in his Land Rover a long distance until they spotted a herd of springboks, an antelope-like animal that was their favorite prey. In a season of extreme game scarcity, the Bushmen's hunt was successful beyond their hopes. They headed back to camp in high spirits, with a buck tied on the roof of the truck.

"If the people back at the camp only knew about this, they would be thrilled," Van der Post remarked to the bushman seated next to him. The bushman looked quizzically at him.

"They know."

When they arrived at the camp, the fires were burning, the pots of precious water were already boiling, and the women were singing a welcoming song.

Later on in the book, van der Post relays a conversation that he had with another bushman, who told him that when they are away from their families and they are needed by them because of some emergency, they feel a "tapping" in their chests.

I realize that I have precious little evidence for this, but I suspect that we might have senses that have become vestigial or perhaps just unfamiliar to us that we seldom utilize or even know of, due to our living in a technologically oriented culture. Our ancestors used these senses, and present-day hunter-gatherers still employ them every day because their very lives may depend upon them. Does the existence of senses that we are unaware of sound unlikely? How do birds navigate thousands of miles across the open sea during their migrations and arrive unerringly at the same nesting spot that they occupied the previous year? Why did elephants break their chains and head for the hills in 2004, just hours before a gigantic tsunami hit the coast of Thailand? How do bats navigate at night and in caves? It took many years before scientists discovered that bats use sonar that they had evolved millions of years before we invented it.

Many years after that class in the Pine Barrens, Lanie and I drove from Idaho to a Boy Scout camp in the Santa Cruz Mountains of northern California in order to retake

Tom's Advanced Tracking and Nature Observation class. We had loved doing it years before because it opened us up to a lot of new and unexpected experiences and insights. Not surprisingly, the material he was covering now was almost completely different from the last time. Tom had a way of doing that with his advanced courses. In fact, we had banked on that.

"I want you to go out to your sit spots now and memorize everything you see in it," Tom Brown drawled with a smirk. Whenever I saw that crooked smile form on Tom's face, I knew that we were in for trouble. "You've got only one hour. You better get going."

There you go again, Tom, I thought, asking us to do something that is impossible, stretching the limits of what we think we know, again.

I headed on the double up the hill, toward a small glade in the forest that I had been using all week in which to meditate and do all kinds of other psychological gymnastics. I knew the place well by now but not nearly well enough for this task. I entered and sat down facing inward on a large, rough bark log near the entrance. Of course, I recognized many of the trees and bushes. They felt like old friends because I had come there so often. The spot was typical of California hill country, with trees such as manzanita and Australian pine, pine bushes, flowers and various grasses that I recognized and had even put names on, but to memorize them all? And what their form was? And where they were located relative to other landmarks? And in one hour?

This is crazy, I thought, It's like trying to learn a whole new language in one day. Then I got to work.

I looked around the leafy glade. How could I even attempt to memorize what it looked like? There must be hundreds of things here, many with dozens of parts. Enough of this doubting. Let's begin, I again urged myself. I started systematically, like the scientist I am. First the trees, where were they? What were their leaves like? How many limbs? How twisted and branched? I progressed from there to the bushes, grasses, rocks and twigs lying on the ground, and even the color and texture of the soil itself. Midway through, I felt as though my head would burst from absorbing all this information. Then, I decided for about the third time, to just let go of my thoughts about the enormity of my task and continued by observing and memorizing the different kinds of grasses. How many blades?

Some time later, still totally absorbed in what I was doing, I barely heard the faint signal to come back, a crow's call relayed up the hill. I had finished my compilation just in time. On my way to the dining hall where the class met, I saw other, quiet, seemingly bemused and preoccupied classmates drifting back alongside me. We did not talk or even acknowledge each other's presence. It was as if we were afraid that doing so would spill all of the information we had just gathered, as if it were a bowl of soup, too hot to handle.

As we sat in the hall, Tom, late as usual, mounted the stage. OK, what gimmick was he going to pull now? It was almost always the unexpected. He told us to lie down, close our eyes, and go through the now familiar exercise, designed to put us in a more or less meditative state.

"Now, visualize your sit spot. See it all, every pebble,

every twig." He gave us some time to do this and finally spoke again.

"Now, where are the claw marks of the mice on the tree bark? Where are the deer tracks on the ground? Take a moment. Locate them."

Now, he had finally done it. This was truly ridiculous. Nevertheless, in my mind's eye, I hastily scanned my sit spot. There were no mouse scratching on the trees! I was getting angry. I felt that I was being led by the nose and made a fool! There were no deer tracks, none at all! Wait a minute! There, on the ground, not 24 inches in front of my feet were two perfect deer tracks. Now, I must be having hallucinations. I could not have missed seeing those tracks right in front of my real eyes, just a half hour ago!

Tom's voice interrupted my inner dialog.

"Now, go back to your sit spots and prove it," he thundered.

Reluctantly, grumbling, I dragged myself up the hill again, sat down on the log and tried to compose myself. Finally, I gazed down in front of me. There, on the ground, two feet ahead of me, were two close-together, perfect deer tracks.

All right, I thought, what is the explanation for this? How could I have missed it? It was right in front of me! All kinds of crazy ideas rushed through my head. Could Tom have sent some of his instructors to our secret spots to make track impressions with a deer foot while we were in the dining room? If so, how could he or she have known exactly where to plant the tracks? Not only did they not know where I imagined the tracks to be, but also they did not even know where my secret spot was. I rejected my bout of paranoia. Slowly, the truth dawned on me. I must have seen those tracks previously but did not consciously register it. There were deer tracks and mouse clawings all over the camp. The place was positively lousy with them. One of the other guys, who had his spot farther up the hill, had even found the pugmarks of a mountain lion in his spot. He quickly switched spots.

Tom had taught us yet another lesson. Our memories are prodigious, much greater than we imagine. We must constantly be absorbing information on some level that under average circumstances does not even reach our conscious minds. But it is there and accessible to us under special circumstances.

### *True Lostness*

This feat of memory reminded me of another Laurens van der Post anecdote. He was talking to two Bushmen, all of them trying to exchange information, by learning some of each other's language. He came to the word, "lost." The Bushman looked puzzled. They did not get it. The word did not appear to have a !Kung equivalent. He struggled to get the concept across. Suddenly, these two burst out laughing and literally rolled around on the ground, holding their bellies.

"Laurens, did I not know," they explained, when the burst of merriment died down, "that there was not a tree, expanse of sand or bush that was alike? How could anyone, even a European, possibly get lost?"

Of course, you can get lost in different ways. This

disconnect from nature is evident all around us. The Conoco service station a mile and a half down the road from me, on the corner of U.S. Highway 95, has a surprisingly nice restaurant, and we sometimes walk down there for breakfast. The floor-to-ceiling glass windows in back of the restaurant show a view of a manicured lawn sloping down to a small lake, surrounded by cattails and other wild marsh plants. Many red-winged blackbirds hang around the reeds, while wild geese, duck and mergansers cavort on the water. Every once in a while, a blue heron appears, flying over the pond. A gentle, grassy hill rises in back of the lake and much farther in back of it, hanging in the distance like a shimmering mirage, are the brilliantly white, rugged snow covered granite peaks of the Selkirk Mountains that extend north into Canada.

We were sitting at a table in the restaurant one sunny Sunday, not too long ago, watching this beautiful scene while a little boy, about 3 years old, frolicked on the lawn and was watched by a matronly woman, whom I took to be his grandmother. He was having a grand time racing around the lawn, going down a children's slide and running around a small faux waterfall, among large rocks that had been set there by a landscaper.

This rather formal garden ended abruptly in another 20 feet or so, where the carefully trimmed lawn was bordered by wildflowers, grasses and all sorts of wild plants, on land that gently sloped down about 50 yards to some very large cottonwood trees. Farther on, the marshes started and then came Walsh Lake. This wild scene obviously attracted the child, but every time he approached the end of the lawn, Grandma swooped down upon him and turned him back. This action, which after a while began to resemble a choreographed dance between the two, was repeated dozens of times. The boy was clearly entranced by the wildness beyond the lawn, but Grandma would not even let him stick his toes in such dangerous territory.

I felt sorry for the little tyke and even considered going out there and telling Grandma that there were no rattlesnakes, anacondas or crocodiles in northern Idaho, only harmless garter snakes, birds, zooming dragonflies, along with fluttering white and yellow butterflies. Besides, if a mountain lion came bounding out of the marsh, eager for a tasty little human morsel, we would be sure to spot him far enough away and have plenty of time to sound the alarm. I refrained from doing so, out of my native good sense. After all, she was just preventing this child from getting lost.

This scene stood in contrast to the one that confronted me a few years later as I sat in my green aluminum-and-canvas-folding chair alongside a rustic picnic table. A little boy was handing me an orange salamander with black spots and was earnestly explaining how he had caught it in a nearby pond that he had been investigating with some of the other kids. Well, I thought, wasn't this what they were supposed to do in a more traditional society? The elders, who had plenty of time in contrast to the busy mothers and fathers, could listen to eager stories from excited children turned loose in nature.

We, along with a dozen other people connected with the Twin Eagles school, had driven again from the Idaho Panhandle, this time to attend Jon Young's Art of Mentoring week in the Santa Cruz Mountains of northern

California. Jon, who is an anthropologist, was Tom Brown's first student. We wanted to see how Jon went about creating a community, and here it was happening before our very eyes. Without even thinking of it, we found ourselves participating in this event. How did he do it? It almost seemed magical, but there was a method to this magic, sometimes visible but mostly subterranean. There were, of course, the formal talks at which Jon and the other instructors wrote things on white boards and listed and explained the principles of building community, like the use of music, stories and teaching of skills. But most of the mentoring was accomplished through something called coyote teaching, a classic American Indian technique. This is best illustrated with an example. At the beginning of the week, we had been divided into small, rather autonomous groups, but as we gradually learned, not haphazardly so. Each group was given both practical jobs, such as cleaning the johns, setting tables, et cetera, and more spiritual ones, such as making sure that everyone's needs were taken care of or that stories were told or recreational needs were taken care of. Was someone wandering around the camp looking lost or forlorn and not participating? Chat with them, find out what troubled them and let the instructors know so that they could try to do something to rectify the situation. Did we need some games and activities? Invent some and involve people in them.

We found out as we went along that each group had been carefully selected to balance age, gender and experience.

Our biggest surprise though came on the last day, when all the groups had been gathered together in a meadow and the instructors were asked to stand to receive recognition for their efforts. We were dumbfounded when we saw that along with the ones we knew to be instructors, one person in each group stood up. They had been planted there in the beginning to gently nudge us in particular directions. Coyote teaching indeed!

## *My Name Is Barry Moses*

One of the American Indians who often comes to Twin Eagles functions is Barry Moses of the Spokane Tribe. Barry is a smiling, cherubic man who looks to be in his 30s but must be older because he has two grown children. He introduces us to the rituals and traditions that his tribe has charged him to learn and pass on to future generations. Barry's story is in part an all too familiar one of American Indians who were "bad boys," growing up in a broken culture and getting into drugs and alcohol. Somehow, Barry overcame this difficult phase of his life and, with the help and support of his tribal elders, has become a remarkable leader.

Barry's overriding concern is the preservation and passing on of his tribe's culture, which is in danger of disappearing. The question, therefore, arises as to why he spends considerable time and energy bringing these traditions to non-Indian groups like ours. To explain this dichotomy, he shared a personal story with us one day. As background, I should tell you that Barry has been accused by some tribal members with betraying his traditions by exporting them to those "blue eyes." Their typical argument is that these people have taken almost everything away from us, our lands, our livelihoods, our language. They even forced our children to attend schools far away, at which our language was banned. What little we have left are our traditions, rituals and religious practices. Now, they want to steal these, too, and you Barry, are aiding and abetting them. These criticisms cut particularly deep with Barry because his wife is a non-Indian, and his grown children have chosen non-Indian mates. That means that his grandchildren will be only one-quarter Indian, and by the rules of his tribe, their children might not be considered tribal members. This situation has weighed on him considerably.

One night, he had a strange dream. In it, he is wandering alone over a landscape of rolling and sere hills with few trees. It looks familiar to him, not like his reservation, but more like the rolling plains over which his people wandered for eons in their hunter-gatherer lifestyle before being confined to that reservation. He feels sad, very lonely and disconnected. After a while, though, he thinks that he hears familiar chanting and drumming, and when he comes over a rise, he sees in the distance, in a hollow of this vast landscape, a group of people who appear to be dressed in traditional American Indian clothing who are singing and dancing. This gladdens his heart, and he hurries down the slope to join them, but something is wrong about this scene. As he approaches these people, he realizes that although they are dressed in traditional costume and are chanting and singing age-old songs, they are not American Indians. He begins to get angry. He feels that they have no right to do this and reproaches their leader, a tall, slim young man with long, braided, yellow hair and flashing blue eyes.

"You are just playacting. You have no right to do this because you are not Indians!"

"Yes, we are," the young man calmly replies.

"Oh, is that so!" Barry shoots back at him. "I know everyone in my tribe. What is your name?"

The young man looks at him and says, "My name is Barry Moses."

## Wilderness Immersion

Perhaps a dozen people were gathered in a circle in the middle of a large yurt, and there was a merry fire crackling in the wood stove in the corner. As I looked around, I could not but smile at what a motley crew we made. Most of these people were in their long winter underwear and other stages of undress because they had just come indoors from a raging blizzard. It was also obvious that there was a big gap in our ages here. About a half dozen of my companions were fresh-faced, red-cheeked twentysomethings, men and women, all standing, laughing, conversing and glowing from their realization that they had just had accomplished something wonderful. They had returned alive and well from the top of a mountain in a winter snowstorm. There were a few of us standing there, though, who were probably thanking their lucky stars that we had not been on that mountain with them. We did not have to test ourselves that way because as acknowledged elders, we had paid our dues long ago and were being accorded seats of honor at this celebration.

*Wilderness Immersion Students – Tim Corcoran*

When Lanie and I first became associated with Twin Eagles, we found it more than a little bit disconcerting that we were always given the front row seats at festivities and that no one else would eat or even stand in line to get food until we had filled our plates. Frankly, I resented it at first. After all, I thought, we are neither cripples nor children and did not require special privileges. After a while, though, it dawned on us that this was the way traditional peoples treated their elders. They thought we deserved this treatment because we had not only survived to such advanced ages but had undoubtedly garnered much wisdom in our journeys through life. Over time, I grew to understand that these traditions were important, not only for us but for the other, mostly younger participants. This was an acknowledgement of our experience and accumulated wisdom. Traditional peoples revere their elders, and that was not a bad thing to teach youngsters in our culture too.

Most of the young people gathered in the yurt this day were Wilderness Immersion students, engaged in a year-long, grueling, intense and finally exhilarating program overseen by Tim Corcoran and Jeannine Tidwell, the heads of the Twin Eagles Wilderness School. One of the fresh-faced people standing there and laughing was their junior instructor, Daniella, a compact and dynamic woman from British Columbia, who despite her seeming youth, had been teaching wilderness skills for the last 10 years. The other, Daniel, was a tall, slim, thirtysomething with a scruffy red beard and a twinkle in his eyes, who had a wonderful gift of music, singing and playing the guitar. I had watched him grow at Twin Eagles from an uncertain and hesitant stripling into an assured and accomplished leader. He was also the son of white-bearded-but-sinewy-muscled David, who was one of the elders present at this gathering, and their relationship was a good example of the passing of knowledge, skill and commitment from one generation to another.

The Wilderness Immersion Program is a wilderness skills and community building program at Twin Eagles that is designed to bring these young people into a closer relationship with Nature and their authentic selves. It will send them out as mature, dedicated teachers who will help others, especially children, to reconnect with Earth.

Their areas of study covered such topics as wilderness survival, tracking, ethno botany and naturalist training, but a description like that does not give an adequate notion of how the training is accomplished. The school's philosophy and training is based on American Indian teachings and traditions, some of which is done by bringing in guest instructors from various tribes such as the Spokane, Sioux and Ojibwa. These American Indians are mostly practitioners of that mysterious teaching that I previously mentioned, which Jon Young dubbed coyote mentoring. It is a subtle way of teaching people who are often not aware that they are being taught.

To illustrate this method, Jon once told us that after years of camping as a kid with this peculiar fellow, Tom Brown, who seemed to know nothing and was always asking Jon loads of infuriatingly naive questions about what he had seen and done, Tom had asked him to teach at his Tracker School. Jon was astonished. He thought, What can this guy teach? He knows nothing. Jon soon discovered that Tom knew a few million things about survival and wilderness awareness and had been engaged in coyote mentoring him all those years.

We were holding a celebration in this yurt. Three days ago, the young people gathered here in the yurt had started out from a trailhead in the middle of the winter in the Selkirk Mountains of northern Idaho, dragging sleds loaded all their gear, food and fuel enough for three days up a mountain in a winter storm. How they got there, dug a snow cave large enough to shelter eight people, cooked and ate meals, squabbled and cooperated, failed and triumphed, and got back down with both their skins and souls intact, were the subjects of their stories, which we elders had come to hear and celebrate.

Anna, the giggler, aka the "bird woman," due to her affinity for and knowledge of our feathered friends, is a curvy, red-headed young woman, who told us of pulling her sled up that mountain until the sweat soaked through her thermal underwear and into her outer clothing. Only halfway up after hours of toil, she began to stumble over and over again. Finally, she fell exhausted with her face in the snow, unable to move another inch. Then she told us of getting up, inch by inch, first on her hands, then on her knees and finally on her feet, and pulling that damn sled again until she had gotten it all the way up the mountain.

Brian, a thin, short and gentle young man with black-rimmed glasses and 5 o'clock shadow, spoke of working furiously with the others just before twilight to complete the seemingly impossible task of digging a snow cave large enough for eight people, then falling asleep totally exhausted deep inside of it on an icy shelf. He woke in the middle of the night, feeling claustrophobic and having to scramble over his companions' bodies to get outside and breath the free, cold night air. He looked up at the night sky and found the stars to be so brilliant that they were intoxicating.

His companion, elfin and perpetually smiling Alex, told a story of driving herself to exhaustion and feeling humiliated because she could not make it all the way by herself. She had to ask for help from her companions, which she got from them without so much as a grumble or raised eyebrow on their part. She felt partly humbled, relieved and thrilled to be part of such a caring and together group.

Later that day, when the group togetherness had disintegrated while they were trying to build the crucial snow cave, it was Alex who called them together, told them what to do and rallied them to the task. It was in this way that she discovered the hitherto hidden leadership power she had within her.

After listening to many of their stories, we elders were invited to give them feedback. Lanie said that the whole group's personal barriers had seemed to her like an enormous rock face blocking the end of a trail – a real dead-end. But then an arch opened up in the rock, which became a tunnel they walked right through. They each had figuratively seen the same thing at the end of the tunnel: a beautiful, wide-open valley, accessible in all directions.

As I listened to their stories, my heart was filled with immense love and admiration for these young people, and for their courage and determination in overcoming their personal barriers. I could see that they will be infinitely better prepared to face the inevitable fiery furnaces that we must all pass through than I was at their ages. Oh, I said to myself, If I were 40 years or even 30 years younger, I would enroll in the Wilderness Immersion program at Twin Eagles Wilderness School, just to experience all that fun, adventure and growth.

Lanie leaned over and whispered to me, "These are our grandchildren."

Yes, they are, and they might just be able to save the Earth.

# ACKNOWLEDGMENTS

I thank Cassie Dunn Faggion for her help in designing this book, Billie Jean Gerke for doing the copy editing, Chris Bessler, head of Keokee Co. Publishing, Inc. and Christine Holbert, the publisher of Lost Horse Press, each of whom gave me timely advice and needed encouragement.

I particularly want to thank my wife, Lanie Johnson, who provided one of her calligraphic art pieces for the book cover and who created the drawings for the chapter headings. It was her patience, support and faith in my ability that enabled me to complete this book.

Tom Brown Jr. of Tom Brown Tracker, Inc., put me on the right path. Daniel Quinn, author of Ishmael, set my hair on fire about changing our culture, and Jon Young showed me how contemporary Earth-connected communities could be created.

I have also been fortunate to have the help and support of Jeannine Tidwell and her husband, Tim Corcoran, leaders of the Twin Eagles Wilderness School, and powerful influences in helping people to reconnect with Earth. I have also gained wisdom from David Kirchhof of Medicine Circle and Robert Douglas with whom I have had the honor of serving on the Twin Eagles Elders Council.

Barry Moses, who is the historian of the Spokane tribe, is a powerful voice for American Indian traditions and spirituality. His association with Twin Eagles has afforded me the opportunity to experience his wisdom and hear about his extraordinary dreams.

I have also been fortunate to be associated with a wonderful, tireless and selfless group of wolf advocates. I salute, Ann Sydow, Nancy Taylor of The Wolf People, the well-named Bill Howell, Richard Hurry and Merlin Nelson for their work with the Northern Idaho Wolf Alliance (NIWA). I appreciate the efforts of Suzanne Stone, the Idaho representative of Defenders of Wildlife, and her former associate, Jesse Timberlake. Thank you, Doug Honnold of Earth Justice and Brett Haverstick of Speak for Wolves, for your efforts to protect wolves, and to Valerie Bittner who has provided her legal advice and friendship in many of these efforts.

Talking of natural and Earth-friendly communities, the people who make up the Society of Primitive Technology (SPT) and who sponsor the Rabbitstick and Wintercount primitive skills rendezvous have provided a home away from home for Lanie and me for many years. They continually demonstrate that it is possible for humankind to live in an Earth-friendly way. I wish I could personally thank you all but only have room to mention a few SPT individuals who have touched our lives. Paula and David Wescott are the leaders and inspiration for these gatherings. Carrie and Mike Ryan not only keep things humming during the gatherings but also provide inspiration for us in the traditional way they have brought up their family.

Digger Crist, thank you for being my friend and for showing me by your lifestyle how to live on friendly terms with the Earth. Jim Riggs, you helped start it all. Norm Kidder, I will never forget your baskets and never learn half of your knots. Dave Holladay, just keep tapping away on those rocks and helping kids. Dick Baugh, you are the most inventive primitive engineer I know. Estabon, keep those pots burning, and "Duckman," keep those roast ducks cooking. Tom Elpel, I enjoy our talks and admire what you are doing to educate us. Albert Abril, I always look forward to seeing your friendly face at these shindigs. John Kallas, you have enriched us with you knowledge of plants, but I think you went too far in your scientific explorations when you tasted poisonous water hemlock. Cat Farneman, thanks for all the herbal remedies that keep my hay fever at bay during Rabbitstick.

Lynx Vilden, your Living Wild group is a wonder and you are an exemplar at teaching primitive group living. Cody Lundin is a survival instructor at the Aboriginal Living Skills School in Prescott, Arizona, an integral part of these gatherings and the irreverent author of books on how to survive in style.

I learned not only how to make an atlatl and American Indian flute from Bob Kitch but how to patiently teach primitive skills. Mike Powell, the beautiful mountain man capote that you showed me how to cut and sew together still keeps me warm on cold, snowy outdoor evenings and one of these days I will even finish it.

Many thanks also to Jeff "Roadkill" Damm, who always seems to bring some strange and wonderful meat for us to eat at Rabbitstick. Mors Kochansky, of Karamat Wilderness Ways in Canada, is an encyclopedic expert at winter survival and has enlightened us in many ways at the rendezvous.

Randy Russell, of Soulore, helps kid grow into young adults, not an easy thing, as many parents will attest. Thank you for being my friend all these years and supporting my educational efforts.

Last but not least, I want to thank some young men and women who have assisted me in these efforts and whom I have watched grow into strong, confident adults. I am pleased to count Joshua Walters, Kristofer Yamada, Jesse Hoag, Daniella Roze, who has recently established the Thriving Roots Wilderness School in British Columbia, Qwalen Berntsen, Finan Meschke, Matthew Peck, aka the "Lake Monster," Daniel Kirchhof, along with Alex Kiersky and her husband, Brian, who are among my many collaborators and friends.

I owe a special debt of gratitude to my friends at the Sandpoint Chapter of the Idaho Writers League who were always willing to listen to and read my writing, and especially for their ability to critique it gently without crushing my spirit and to continually encourage my efforts. Thanks particularly go to: Mary Haley, Jim Payne, Janice Able and Tom Reppert of our Tuesday night critique group, and my special thanks to our poet laureate, Linda Rubin, whose sweet words of encouragement were, well, like poetry to me.

# CITED BOOKS AND PUBLICATIONS

*Childhood and Society* – Erik Erikson
*The Cave of Forgotten Dreams* – Werner Herzog
*Collapse* – Jared Diamond
*98.6 Degrees: The Art of Keeping Your Ass Alive* – Cody Lundin
*Ishmael* – Daniel Quinn
*The Great Dance* – Craig and Damon Foster
*The Immense Journey* – Loren Eiseley
*The Star Thrower* – Loren Eiseley
*The Songlines* – Bruce Chatwin
*Stanley and Africa* – Burton and Speke
*Indian Legends of the Pacific Northwest* – Ella E. Clark
*The Messengers of the Gods* – James Cowan
*Journals of Lewis & Clark*
*Last Child in the Woods* – Richard Louv
*Lost World of the Kalahari* – Lorens van der Post
*Native American Ceremony of Giving Thanks* – Jake Swamp
*Nature and the Human Soul* – Bill Plotkin
*Other Peoples' Myths* – Wendy Doniger O'Flaherty
*The Tracker* – Tom Brown, Jr.
*Travels of William Bartram* – William Bartram

# CONTACTS

**Ancient Pathways To A Sustainable Future**
http://ancientpathwaystoasustainablefuture.org

**Barry Moses**
http://sulustu.blogspot.com

**Charles Benbrook**
http://csanr.wsu.edu/author/cbenbrook/

**Ignacio Chapela**
http://bit.ly/25OujoQ

**Arpad Pusztai**
http://bit.ly/1sxQKWv

**Idaho Fish and Game**
http://fishandgame.idaho.gov

## Ishmael.org

http://www.ishmael.com/welcome.cfm

## Jon Young's Art of Mentoring

http://8shields.com/programs/art-of-mentoring/

## Ken Fischman

http://ancientpathwaystoasustainablefuture.org

## Rabbitstick Primitive Skills Rendezvous

http://backtracks.net/RSWC.html

## Speak for Wolves 2016

http://www.speakforwolves.org

## Tracker Wilderness Survival School

https://www.trackerschool.com

## Twin Eagles Wilderness School

http://www.twineagles.or

# INDEX

# INDEX

Made in the USA
San Bernardino, CA
26 October 2016